The Spirit
of
Trees

PETER WEST

GREEN MAGIC

GREEN MAGIC
53 Brooks Road
Street
Somerset
BA16 0PP
England
www.greenmagicpublishing.com

Designed and typeset by Carrigboy, Wells, UK
www.carrigboy.co.uk

ISBN 9781739973339

GREEN MAGIC

Contents

Introduction

Without trees, the human race would not survive for long. Trees did not exist many millions of years ago, at least, not as we know them today, but then nor did human life either. The tree we see today is a fairly simple affair and quite unlike the very first growths back in the Devonian Period of around some 450-350 million years ago.

Today, the tree we know and see has allowed us to find out how, where and why it grows as it does. It employs a reasonably simple process. The trunk is usually a single round shaft that is made up of a multitude of wood strands called *xylem*. They carry the water they need from their many roots to the branches, fruit and leaves. New xylem grows in rings at the outer edge of the trunk, just behind the bark. This helps to add to the girth and allows the plant to grow taller. We have learned how to decipher this information in order to assess the age that the tree has reached.

This is not quite how those ancient trees grew. Today, we now have a much better idea of how the present generation of trees grow. However, no matter what period we live in, trees have become extremely important because they have dominated the Earth (and still do so) since those very early times. They helped to create the first early forests. We now appreciate the way in which they have played such a key role in the natural processes of life. Trees absorb carbon dioxide and other gases from the atmosphere and release oxygen.

By adding this back into to the atmosphere, they affect the climate and influence conditions that fostered the emergence of other life forms. Despite their early critical role in the evolution of life on Earth, these trees of old do not appear to have many modern descendants.

They all seemed to have just vanished around about the end of the Devonian Era. There may have been a variety of reasons for this but it was probably because they lost out in the shade of the taller and more robust growths. It is possible that their ever-changing environmental conditions could also have exerted its effect as well

As a matter of interest, there are some trees called Archaeopteris that a wide variety of tree scientists seem to think probably arrived on the scene a few hundred years later. This more or less goes along with the known facts. Old Mother Nature, when she exerts her influence, she keeps a healthy balance on what lives and dies, and when.

Not many people appreciate how a tree comes into being. Equally, quite a few are quite surprised (astonished might be a better word) to find that one of these huge growths begins as a small seed. For a moment or two, think of the acorn and the massive oak tree, or of the ash, England's tallest tree, and its minute seed – the samara.

Once the seed has begun to fruit, it will send a small shoot above ground level where it will be at its most endangered state. It could be accidentally eaten by a passing animal, especially by a grazing deer or, of course, adverse weather conditions could damage it. Then there is always the chance it could be weak and die naturally.

All things being equal, from here it grows into a sapling which is reckoned at about 35cm or so. Provided all is still well and the sapling suffers no harm, it will gradually grow into a mature tree. Once the mature tree, like the oak, for example, begins to produce fruit and acorns at around 40 years old, it will continue to grow for many more years to come. That is putting everything at its most simplest.

Let's go back to the beginning again. Trees would have sprung up and grown from the multitude of fern-like growths along with the many shrubs and bushes of all kinds that proliferated in those days. If nothing else, trees would have reached for the sky anyway just to survive and that is exactly what they did. From these masses of the various ground-based growths, trees began to form – to stretch and reach ever higher for the light and, of course, for the warmth of the sun.

But what exactly do trees do?

Well, to start with, they work wonders at improving the air quality. They take in all manner of pollutants in through their leaves, filter through whatever could possibly damage anything in the air, other plant life on the ground or other life forms. Basically, this is using their wonderful system of photosynthesis to produce oxygen, without which very little life can exist. Photosynthesis is the way in which the process produces and prolongs much of our green plant life, along with a few other organisms that transform light energy into chemical energy.

Trees help to conserve and preserve this energy, no matter where they are, so that everything living or standing nearby can reap that little extra warmth from the winter sun. This is where the deciduous tree really comes into its own. They lose their leaves in the winter period, thus allowing all and sundry to benefit. People who own their house also appreciate the coniferous trees, for when they place one a slight tad to the north side of the home it will strongly help reduce the chill from the winter wind.

We have also learned that trees planted close to a house, especially in the garden, help to increase the value of the home by as much as 10% or even more in some cases. People who travel out on their shopping exercises have an inclination to stay out longer when there are trees in their shopping malls. This is largely because the air created by the tree makes people feel better. It has also been claimed that some folk might even pay a little more for their goods at such times.

There are also other claims that there are some people who seem to appear more relaxed and easy-going when their streets have trees in them. They tend to go out more often and stay to enjoy a coffee or whatever, especially if there are cafes with outdoor seating and tables.

People forced to stay in hospital enjoy looking at trees from their windows and, it is said, some may even recover back to their normal state quicker than those who cannot see one.

This bears out our knowledge that trees are known to lower the humidity and temperature as well as help to slow down wind speed if it gets too strong. This is probably in the way they influence evaporation away from city centres, which can become so-called "heat islands" in our hotter summer spells. It was found that when trees are planted and allowed to grow in some parking areas they have quite clearly helped to reduce the temperature by as much as 40% or greater.

Perhaps it is even more obvious that no matter where one finds a tree of any kind, there will be more life forms, such as a huge variety of birds and other small creatures living in reasonable safety. The largest non-flying animal life would be the squirrel in the UK. Trees also provide shelter for other much smaller creatures that dwell in the bark or holes they find or make in the growths.

Generally speaking, most ordinary people may not realise or tend to forget that if enough trees have been planted in certain ways, they will help reduce traffic noise by up to some 8 or 9 decibels in places. A group of trees planted out properly with this in mind can also block out any unsightly or unnecessary views.

Efforts like this produce a lot of environmental improvements often without the local populace appreciating it – at first. When it does dawn on some of them, it doesn't take a lot of time and effort for people to get together to ensure these ideas are actively pursued. The trees become well looked after. Curiously, it has also been found that apartment blocks with a high level of tree life around them also helps to reduce criminal activity.

I was brought up in the countryside throughout the 1940's. I lived in a small village called Burghfield, some 10 miles outside the nearest largest town, Reading, in the heart of Berkshire. The house in which we lived was on a corner of three small lanes. We were totally surrounded by tree life of all kinds. On one side we had a huge rookery – a smallish forest entirely taken over and run by a vast swathe of rooks.

They either could not stop or had to permit an infiltration of a lot of other bird life. There were many owls, blackbirds and crows along with quite a community of squirrels and other non-flying animal life. There were also many families of much smaller creatures that included caterpillars, creepy-crawlies and a fairly vast insect world that Mother Nature in her wisdom also allowed.

Opposite the house, and many miles long, were lines of trees that were around ten or twelve deep and in which all manner of life dwelt. On the other side of these roadways were just massive hedgerows that were trimmed back down from time to time by the local farm workers. In those long ago days, they were infested with hedgehogs galore, and a whole host of other small country life. There were many pathways through the trees but there were also masses of more fascinating tracks that attracted youngsters like me and the many equally young friends I had in those times.

Going to school in those days was an adventure bar none. I could walk through the trees, go across two smallish fields also lined with trees, down a small path between a farmhouse and a normal house to get to school. If the weather was really bad, I was taken by road by car, which took longer. Coming home after school took longer as well but then there were many reasons for that. Learning to climb this tree or that, one always took time apart from the many falls. But once having got to an advantage point and looking out over the countryside dreaming or "being" this or that really did take up a lot of a boy's time. My grandmother never started my tea until she actually saw me coming up the drive - wise woman

What I did not know, until many years later, was that I was so engulfed by all this wood and mini forest life that I was actually "forest bathing". This is how the German author Peter Wohlleben (*The Heartbeat of Trees*) describes these forays into the woods to take advantage of all the many benefits. As a rule, many of the older country people knew of the benefits of simply walking or just sitting by the trees. Peter Wohlleben took his interests much further and describes his findings quite succinctly in his book.

Go into a park, a wood or a forest, sit or lay down somewhere and let Mother Nature take over. No matter what age you are now, try it for yourself – but do try to relax. You may not be able to do so properly at first but after a while you will and is then that you will "feel" the differences. You will go back for more, especially living in the kind of smelly old world we do at present.

Thank heaven for the trees!

Named Celebration Trees

In this early part of the second decade of the present century, there are currently some 195 countries that make up the world, all of them bar two are affiliated as member states at one level or another to the United Nations. The two non-member countries which do not or will not belong to this organisation but do, however, send officials to observe proceedings, are the Holy See and the State of Palestine.

The Holy See of Rome, Vatican City, is the apostolic district and home of the Bishop of Rome, the Pope. The fundamental purpose here is to describe the home and capital of the Catholic Church, where the Pope and the Curia exist. Together, they form an international governing system from the Vatican City, with authority over all of the world's Catholic peoples. It was allegedly created by the Saints Peter and Paul, who chose the site in the first century.

In essence, they have no national tree as such, but the enormous decorated Christmas tree erected annually in Saint Peter's Square in front of Saint Peter's Basilica is recognised as the most probable growth.

The State of Palestine offers allegiance to no one and although it recognises the United Nations, it only observes what goes on and does not belong to it. Palestine is governed by the Palestine Liberation Organisation (PLO). Its national tree is the olive tree.

Countless other countries have a listed interest, or have adopted a national tree, some of which really do take some finding. There are far too many to write up here which, for the time being, also goes for the individual states of the USA. They have all listed their state tree, which is much easier to find but, again, there are too many to write up here. Curiously though, the United States, as a whole country, does have a national tree – the oak.

It is interesting to note that the UK, Germany, France and Spain all list the oak as their tree, although in fairness, we here in England (or the UK as a whole) have clearly stated our tree as the Royal Oak. There is no real difference as such. During the English Civil War, one of the men assisting and helping the king, Charles I, advised him that their present location (Boscobel House) was unsafe. The assistant recommended that they seek somewhere else and suggested that he and the king hide in a large oak tree in the woodlands near where they were at the time. The king agreed and they took some food and drink and spent the day in a pollarded oak tree, which then became known as the Royal Oak.

The annual Christmas tree is, perhaps, the most widely recognised named growth in the world – no matter what your religious beliefs may be. It has a fascinating history too. Its origins can be traced back to Egyptian and Roman times when they used to display decorated evergreen branches over their doors and along the walls and window openings, long before Christianity came along.

They did not have 'windows', as we now know them. There would have been some sort of curtaining or coverings over openings in their walls which were there to allow light in and, more than likely, the odour of the home out.

On or about the winter solstice, which falls on the 21st or 22nd of December each year in the northern hemisphere, the ancient Romans held a feast they called the Saturnalia. This was to honour and respect Saturn, their god of agriculture. They were aware that, with the passing of the solstice, farm life of all kinds, including the relevant trees and other plants, would soon be growing again with their fruit and vegetables. Thus, their way of showing their devotion and respect was to decorate their homes and temples with evergreen boughs and branches.

The Egyptians worshipped Ra, a hawk-headed being who wore the sun in his crown. At this time of the year, the sun would have been weak. Ra would have seemed to have been frail and feeble but at the time and turn of the solstice he would have started to look better. Thus did the Saturnalia come about.

In the more northerly parts of Europe, the Druids (the so-called priests of the extremely ancient Celts) also used to decorate their temples with evergreen branches and boughs, which they acknowledged as the symbols of everlasting life. Later, the Vikings pursued similar ideals when they thought that this evergreen life was the special plant of their sun god, Balder.

Much later, it is to Germany we turn for the next phase in this solstice-cum-Christmas use of plant decorating. They would create small pyramids of wood, decorate them with evergreen materials and take them indoors. Some might have used candles if wood for this decorating was hard to come by. Later still, some of these people lit the candles, which is yet another version of the basis for how the Christmas tree was born.

We turn now to the Americans of the early 1830's. Some of the first or earliest Christmas trees were observed in or by the homes of the German settlers of the time. The Americans did not take very kindly to them at all. A few of these trees were seen some 90–100 years earlier in New England Puritan areas, where they were very seriously frowned upon by all and sundry. There were many spoken and written words of condemnation of these "heathen traditions", as one of the then 'almost' established church leaders so forcibly put it.

Even earlier than this, one Massachusetts Court actually passed a decree making an observation of any celebration, other than a church service, to be an offence. Many people were fined for the displaying or hanging of decorations, up until the middle of the nineteenth century. It was about now that hordes of Irish and German immigrants flooded the area and the Puritans were forced to alter their role regarding these events.

In the middle of the nineteenth century, the English ruler, Queen Victoria, allowed her German husband, Prince Albert, to be shown in an early photograph of her – he and her children standing by a then fairly moderately decorated Christmas tree that he, Prince Albert, had obtained for his family. By this time, Queen Victoria had garnered much favour with her subjects and, as the populace of the time were ever willing to jump on the bandwagon, it didn't take long for them to pursue this idea.

Within a very short space of time, tree ornaments and decorations were arriving from the continent and the Christmas tree became most fashionable. Initially, the trees used were about 65cm high until the early twentieth century, when the Americans preferred and used trees that stretched from floor to ceiling.

The Christmas tree had more or less arrived but there were, and still are, a few differences here and there, in respect of celebrations, from country to country. Not all countries use the same type of tree to celebrate.

In Brazil, for example, because it is in the southern hemisphere, Christmas falls in the summer period. Quite a few of the inhabitants tend to cut down a pine tree and dab small pieces of cotton on the branches to simulate the snow of winter.

In Norway, the children are usually banned from the decorating while the parents do this, but then they must join in a tree circle ritual when it is all finished. The family must then all join hands and walk around the tree singing Christmas hymns.

In Ireland, the tree may be decorated with all sorts of different coloured baubles, lights and pieces of tinsel. The house tends to be covered in all manner of candles and garlands, along with holly and ivy. The doors are usually hung with mistletoe and decorative wreaths.

THE NEW YEAR TREE

Often mistaken for a Christmas tree ritual is the Cantonese and Vietnamese act of planting a new growth to mark their new year. Strictly speaking, this is a New Year event and the plant, no matter what it is, is called the New Year Tree. It may be the Nin Fu Bamboo, the Peach Flower (for good relationships) or just a small piece of ordinary bamboo. In some places, the kumquat tree is decorated and used.

In Turkey, the vast majority of the populace are Muslim and they do not celebrate Christmas, but they do mark the turn of each new year with a New Year Tree. Following on from the modernisation of the country, when the Islamic calendar was dispensed with, the Gregorian calendar was introduced in its place. The New Year celebrations began to be pursued in the early 1920's. They became so popular that Christmas trees were brought into the country, but as New Year Trees.

These days, it is the custom for New Year Trees to be put into place at any time between the start of December to the end of January. Presents are exchanged as New Year gifts, and that is now widely recognised as a prime example of the westernised Turkish culture.

It has also been discovered that there were once travelling tribes who were known to pursue an extremely old tradition called *Nardoqan* – another old name for the winter solstice. People would exchange gifts at this time and some authorities are wondering if that was once a part of the very early Christmas festivities.

But it is largely to the Russians that we look to in respect of the New Year Tree. In the last year of the seventeenth century, the then ruler of the country, Peter the Great, decided to take on board European practices in respect of Christmas and the New Year. He decreed in 1699 that the first day of the New Year would fall on January 1st and NOT the first day of September, as had been practised for quite some time.

He made it a law that "... the pine tree, fir and juniper branches will be used to decorate houses and gateways along the main streets ..." It soon took on and became a countrywide affair, although from roughly the middle 1800's onward the authorities in Russia began stronger activities against Christian believers and their pursuits. Today, all children and their families freely celebrate their New Year with a decorated tree as prescribed.

There are other named trees. There is a Spring Planting Tree in some countries; an Easter Tree and a Midsummer Tree in others. Elsewhere, in some other countries there are Harvest Trees planted to celebrate all that has been successfully gathered in. In one or two other areas a November and a December Tree are created for various reasons.

Finally, we must remember the ancient Spanish village of Mondoñedo, which was recorded as being the first place to have held the first documented Arbour Plantation Festival in the world in 1594. Lime and horse-chestnut trees are still planted on that day and a small granite marker along with a bronze plate record that very first time. Arbour Day is still held annually, a day dedicated in many places when public tree planting ceremonies are held in Australia, the United States and many other countries. Arbour Day is usually held on the last Friday in April, but it does differ from place to place, yet again, for a wide variety of probably local reasons. As a rule, the day is celebrated in the last week of April.

Tu BiShvat (Arbour Day in the Jewish calendar) is observed on the 15th day of Shevat, which is the eleventh month of their calendar. The date usually falls in January or February in the UK, which uses the Gregorian calendar. It is not celebrated as a public holiday in the UK but those few Jewish groups that could close may provide a few part services to allow for the festival to occur on the day. Fruits and trees are pushed into a centre place when it becomes the custom to eat lots of fruit on that day, especially associated with areas that Jewish people tend to regard as the Holy Land.

Among these fruits would be barley, dates, grapes, figs, pomegranates, olives and wheat. These are foods that would also feature strongly in the celebratory meals held by Jewish families and communities all around the UK. Another tradition associated with Tu BiShvat is the planting of a tree to help raise funds for charities dedicated to planting trees in Israel.

Also known as the New Year of the Trees, Tu BiShvat is one of four Jewish New Year Days. The other three fall on the first day of Nisan, the first of Elul, and the first day of Tishrei (or Rosh Hashana) in the Jewish calendar. It marks the start of the agricultural period and is used more traditionally as the cut-off date for any levying of the fruits from these trees. There is a National Arbour Day for Wales and Scotland but, so far, nothing appears to be done nationally in Eire.

Creatures of the Forest

One tree, a couple, a small group, wood or forest cannot exist for long without the support of the creatures that dwell within their domain. There are hordes of them, all sizes, styles and types. They all live together relatively peacefully with Mother Nature keeping her watchful eye on them all, thus ensuring the balance is always kept at manageable levels. Some of these species are almost extinct, while others may be very near their limits. For all of them the tree is their home, somewhere where they feel protected and their individual food is plentiful.

There is always a wide range of birds to be found in any tree, some will live there while others may be temporarily sheltering within the branches and leaves which always afford cover for them. There will also be a tremendous range of insects, small mammals and reptiles of all manner of sizes that will all live together either in the trees, under or by them.

One of the most endangered species is the English pine marten. It is about the same size as a squirrel and has a dark fur-like coat. There is usually a small white patch on the throat and they all have a long fluffy tail. They have been almost extinct in England but there are quite a few that live in hollow Scots pine trees in Scotland under the ever watchful eyes of specialist forest rangers.

The stronger pine martens that live in pairs are occasionally released in one or two of our northern forests. One of these areas, Sherwood Forest, has had a number of them for some time now and they all seem to be doing quite well in their new home. As a pure coincidence, it has been observed that where the pine marten is seen to survive, the grey squirrel has almost disappeared. In some Irish areas where the pine marten is surviving, the grey squirrel has virtually vanished. The local conditions seem to have allowed the red squirrel to re-establish itself again.

The grey squirrel was brought to England by one of the dukes of Bedford, Herbrand Russell, who first introduced it into the park at Woburn Abbey in the 1880's. He is also suggested to have allowed a rather large population of the greys into Regents Park in London and Richmond Park in Surrey. This furry, very speedy small creature is a voracious nut eater and a tree climber par excellence. In some areas where it is called a 'tree rat', the grey is an invader no matter where it goes or settles. It doesn't like opposition and carries a disease known as 'squirrel pox', to which it itself seems relatively immune. However, this pox has attacked the red squirrel with ulcers and scabs.

This was one of the reasons the red squirrel moved away from the grey infiltration. The sickness has, until fairly recently, tended to kill off the red squirrel, but a much better result is now showing for these reds. They are surviving more and more and growing much stronger where they do live. The grey has had war declared on it and, since 1937, it has been declared as a pest. Anyone may kill them off, and do, with impunity.

All manner of war has been raged against them and they are very slowly beginning to die off more than ever before. This has encouraged many people to look for and help the native red. However, what many people don't know is that the red is not, strictly speaking, a native animal to these shores. They were introduced by the Romans many centuries earlier.

On a much lighter and, indeed, prettier note; tree life is greatly enhanced by a huge variety of butterflies, bugs, ladybirds and moths in their various stages of evolution. These multi-coloured creatures favour the trees with the broader leaves, but they will live in almost any tree as long as there are leaves under which they can stay hidden. If you stand quite still for long enough, they will emerge and show themselves.

They are all a glorious sight, probably because you rarely see any of them in your garden, although, as a rule, they are probably there but they do keep well away from any possible danger because life is precious. In their earlier stages, they creep about as an absolute horde of caterpillars of all sizes and colours munching their way through the leaves. Take the time to turn one or two of these leaves over and you will see where some will have attached themselves to a leaf and will be weaving a cocoon in a relatively hidden spot, prior to the next stage in their existence.

Look higher up into the trees, especially into the hazels, and you may spot one or two dormice. When there are just a few shells lying about, there won't be many but if there are a lot of empty shells around, expect to see a lot of them. The dormouse is one of the few animals that prefers to hibernate somewhere on the ground, out of sight and out of mind. However, they prefer to nest high up in the tree of their choice, not far from their favoured honeysuckle bark, leaves and hazel nuts. It isn't often that you will see them on their own. Their mate won't be far away and, if you are patient, you will soon see them rollicking around together.

The tawny owl, also known as the beech, ivy or wood owl, prefers to roost high up in its tree in daylight hours. When dusk begins to fall, they will start to swoop and weave within the trees, searching for their food. If you are very lucky, you might see a great spotted woodpecker; they also like to frequent the tree world. If you don't see them, you may hear them, for they will drum on the tree to remind others that where they are now is their territory. Another of the woodpecker species is the green woodpecker, and this can often be seen in UK gardens, picking at and eating small fruits directly from the trees.

In most heavily wooded areas, there will be a huge range of bats. One of them, Bechstein's bat, lives, hunts and mates deep in the tree world and prefers to make its home in the older trees. Another, the Barbastelle, is also rarely seen but then it also hunts in much the same way as the Bechstein. There are many others, all noted in some way for the way they may sound, hunt or fly. They almost all come out in the late evening as dusk falls or wait for the real dark of the night.

There are well over 600 types of tree-dwelling spiders. One of the cleverest is the crab spider. It can and does change its appearance to suit where it is. With this gift of brilliant camouflage, nothing or no one, especially their prey, know they are there until it is too late. It is not unlike the wolf spider in that is does not spin a web but actually hunts for its food. Web spinners are everywhere, in the trees, on the ground, near small bushes, shrubs and ferns. Their webs, both old and new, proliferate all over the place and you will see the evidence of this, more often than not, just after dawn when they are seen in the early dew. Feeding almost always on insect life, they choose to attack creatures smaller than themselves.

There are other creatures who will venture only so far into any wood or forest area, but who still hunt for their prey in the grounds. The fox and the badger both hunt at night and, while the badger is rarely seen in daylight hours, foxes are often seen hunting or just plain gambolling during daytime. You may also spot a hare or two bouncing about here and there, and rabbits always seem to abound everywhere. However, they are not usually to be seen unless you remain quite still for a while. If there is no disturbance, the rabbits will soon be seen running hither and thither with their partners or their young.

The much smaller field vole will be seen occasionally but they are not easy to spot partly because there aren't very many of them these days. The wild but usually shy hedgehog tends to keep within easy reach of its territory and will stop whatever it may be up to instantly if the feel of any threat is likely. As a rule they are more often to be seen close to the edge of a wood or forest. They tend to not delve too far in because they usually don't know the area as well as they should.

Also, a quite small and rarely seen animal is the yellow-necked mouse. More likely to be spotted in the southern areas of the UK, this little creature seems to spend most of its time keeping an eye open for trouble. It is quite agile and, if or when necessary, will be quite an acrobat in its efforts to get out of trouble. It will leap from branch to branch or even tree to tree if it has to. A distant relative, the hazel dormouse, is acutely endangered and rarely seen but they love the outer reaches of the local tree world where they will hunt and play quite happily. You will almost never see them go home, for they keep that quite secret for obvious reasons.

The lynx, currently extinct here in the UK, is a solitary and avid hunter that may yet be returned to our country by advocates of their future, where there are still a reasonable number of survivors. One of their distant relatives, the Scottish wildcat is a rugged character to be seen prowling around Scottish wooded areas, protecting and hunting within its territory. Alas, it too is an endangered species. What few are left prefer to forage in and around the more remote tree world. As a result, we normal humans rarely see them but specialist forest rangers are well aware of where they are at all times. Equally wild and definitely unfriendly is the stoat. It rarely shows any fear of anything. It is known and has been seen to take on animals several times their own size at times. It is known to climb trees or even burrow quite deeply underground when seeking food.

When we turn away from the normal tree areas to investigate the streams and rivers that meander their way through these wooded regions, the animal life takes on a completely new perspective altogether. Here, a whole new world opens up. In addition to these waterways, there will almost certainly be one or two natural ponds created over long periods of time. These would be fairly regularly topped up by the fairly frequent showers nature ensures, just to keep the balance fairly even at all times.

The small common pond skater will always be seen 'gliding' or 'skating' over the surface of such a pond, occasionally in still ditch water or other very slow-moving waterways. It is predatory, feeding on even smaller insect life by detecting the vibrations they make in the water's surface. There will also be the water boatmen on the surface of the water when there is some algae present. Even if you don't see them, the boatmen will be there. They are vegetarians and the only reason they want to visit these pools is to eat the algae, which is the main food source in their diet. These bugs do appear to be like beetles and can easily be mistaken for cockroaches by those who are not familiar with this insect.

Where there is water of any kind, there will also be frogs, tadpoles and other reptilian life. Frogs will explore the local riverside areas, looking for all manner of food and other matter. They do forage but, while they do so, they are always aware of the possibility of the predators that are rarely far away.

Also moving around in these areas will be the bank vole. This is a rather tubby creature that waffles around, foraging in the woodland and other dense vegetation at the foot of the trees. It searches for and voraciously munches down on various fungi and any fallen blackberries, which it absolutely adores. This vole has rather large ears that are always raised up on the alert for predators, especially the fox and the kestrel.

Often referred to as the architect of the animal world, the beaver will haunt these waters and the local vicinity. Known for their ability to build dams, in doing so, they also create whole new areas because of these talents. Other animal life tends to follow them into these new territories, especially if their food has become a tad scarce.

The ever wily fox is a survivor par excellence. One can see them either carefully heading toward prey or gambolling happily through the woodlands or even out in the open at times. Its diet is quite varied and consists mainly of beetles, birds, rabbits and rats, along with anything else that falls foul of its many and clever hunting talents. Alternatively, they can also be seen walking calmly down any street they choose, looking for food the easy way, via our dustbins. They also openly visit waterways to drink their fill when they feel the urge to do so.

Where there is water, there will be snakes. Fortunately, here in the UK we only have three – the adder, sometimes called a viper (our only poisonous one), along with the grass snake and the smooth snake. The adder is slightly greyish with a zigzag pattern along its back. The female is usually a little lighter in colour. They are a smallish animal, around some 70cm long and they relish all woodland areas. It is the UK's only venomous snake but its poison is of little danger to healthy humans. Although its bite can be very painful and cause an inflammation, it is only dangerous to the very young, the ill or the elderly.

The grass snake is of a varied greenish hue with a black and yellow collar. They are more often seen in wetland, woodland or grassy ground. It can grow quite long, sometimes as much as 140cm or so. They will also be seen in gardens where they like to lay their eggs in our compost bins. The smooth snake is a tad darker than an adder but slightly longer, around 65cm or so. It usually prefers the heath land but it is often seen in the outer woodland territory.

And so we come to the deer. The large and majestic red deer that one expects to see more out in the open grassy places actually prefers the woodland and tree world and is just one of the many different varieties of deer. Normally a peaceful creature, they all dislike change of any kind and prefer to be left alone. It is most unwise to approach any of the herd during the rutting season. They can, will and do inflict a lot of damage and pain on those who dare.

There are many other animals that dwell in the wetlands and woodlands, especially abroad. Depending on where you may be, you could come up against an alligator or a crocodile, some of which really are quite large. Then there are the tree-dwelling snakes, ranging from the smaller deadly poisonous variety to those who prefer to throttle you. In some places, there will be a variety of monkey life that like to swing their way through the branches.

In parts of the southern hemisphere, there is the koala bear that loves trees and climbs all over them all the time.

Some forest areas are where jaguars are known to frequent. The chances of you stepping on one at any time is quite remote, probably because if you ever got that close it would be having you for its next meal.

It is imperative that woodlands, wetlands and forests all over the world are left alone to be preserved by those who know how. Trees benefit the health of us all, for over 20 species of them have some medicinal properties. Just being in among them does all of us the world of good. They benefit all manner of wildlife, many of whom do the same to them by just existing among their growth.

Trees help to benefit the future of us all. They help shape the economy, whereby employers have a healthier work area where their people can visit the parks and trees if they are nearby.

We must protect ourselves by looking after the future of all the trees near us. We are already easing back on what we use for building and printing and we are planting woodlands and forest lands just about everywhere we are in the world.

In this day and age of sudden and or extreme weather, trees will continue to prevent flooding by absorbing huge amounts of storm waters, and they help to reduce wind speeds and absorb carbon dioxide as a matter of course every day. They provide food at all times, dead or alive, because when any tree does fall, it eventually becomes a supplier of a range of fossil fuels like oil, carbon and coal.

Makes you think, doesn't it?

Garden Trees

It is imperative that you ensure any tree in your garden or on land that you own does not impose anywhere close to a neighbour's property. In addition, it is equally as important that you do not place any growth too close to any other adjoining property or, indeed, another building of you own.

Initially, of course, you would not plant any growth that close. However, something may have been planted long before you took over the land. Many years ago, people so often failed to realise just how high a tree might grow or to where the roots might reach. You really do need to heed the likely height and spread that a tree, or any other growth, is likely to attain. In time, any possible overhang could restrict light or, perhaps, prevent the neighbour from what he or she might want to plant or sow. Few people appreciate that trees really do multiply or extend quite beyond belief in some cases.

There are legal positions and restrictions in both cases and they may also apply to other neighbouring trees that overhang the property you own. If, for example you want to cut back or remove branches that overhang your garden from your next-door neighbour's tree, you must first enquire of them if they are prepared to cut them back first. Should they decline and the tree is not protected by what is known as a 'Tree Preservation Order' (TPO) then you may legally prune it – but be reasonable.

You can make any cutback on your side of any joint boundary, be it a fence or a hedge, but you are not permitted to trespass on to his or her property without their permission. You are expected to offer what you do prune back to them first. If they don't want any of it then it becomes your responsibility to clear it away properly. Nothing may be left in their garden without their say so.

If the tree you have has a TPO or is in a conservation area, you must approach the local council for their permission before you do anything. You ought to be able to find out this information from your local archives. There is almost no legal protection in respect of any loss of light that may be caused by a deciduous tree or trees and what there is applies only to the windows of the actual property and not the garden. However, should your hedge be an overly high evergreen hedge, then the local authority has certain powers to instruct a hedge owner to reduce its height or face a fine.

So, what exactly is a tree?

One or two trees can seem like shrubs because parts of the growths have been trained to look like a small tree with a single stem or several stems that branch from ground level. A pollarded tree is one that has had its branches cut back close to the trunk or has been coppiced, that is, cut from near ground level every few years to restrict the size and more or less given a new shape. A tree may be subjected to topiary or cut into a small compact ornamental shape, like a wall shrub might be, as if it were a small tree grown flat against a sheltered wall. The reader will now understand that a 'tree', therefore, may be a growth as opposed to a plant in the most simple of terms. It may grow and grow and grow, or it may remain at a reasonable height year in and year out, depending upon what it is and how it is looked after.

HOW TO LOOK AFTER YOUR TREES

First of all, what type of tree are you about to put in and, more importantly, where? You should place a tree where you know it will grow quite happily for many years. If you should want to move house a few years later on, you may not be able to get at it. So, in a case like this, if you do have some idea, the best bet is to plant the tree in a large pot some 2–6 or even 10 litres in size, depending on the tree.

It will grow in there quite happily for around ten years or so. You can then take it with you when you do go. Always use some of the topsoil from your present garden mixed in with a small amount of peat-free compost, shortly before you do actually change house.

When looking for somewhere to place a tree or trees in your new house grounds, take the time to think things through well before you put anything anywhere. Whatever else you do, you should never just plant trees willy-nilly close to the house or any other of your walls. The roots will eventually interfere with the house foundations sometime later on. Different tree types prefer different conditions. Some might need to be in full sun, full shade or partial shade, or in soils that are loamy, chalky or clay-based.

When you first get your tree, any tree, it is most important that you remove all the wrapping as soon as you can. Then add a small amount of water into the plastic bag that has almost certainly been put around the root system. Try to keep your new tree roots moist and away from direct sunlight until you are ready to plant it. Try to do this as soon as you can. In the meantime, however, it never hurts to keep it in a pot until you are ready to place it where you think it will survive the best.

Try to plant all new trees, irrespective of their particular type, sometime between October and April, that is, from late winter to mid-spring to get the best results. Trees are wonderful additions to any garden and they may well last hundreds of years with the right help.

Should you plant in the spring, you will need to take very special care because the tree may have already started to bud early or grow and form fresh leaves. While deciduous trees come back each year, your tree may not be of this type, so it should be planted quickly in a prepared place, after which, the area must be thoroughly watered. In sunny spring weather a deciduous tree can often bud much earlier than expected. Yet again, the summer is not a good time to plant out any tree, for they really do need all their natural energies to grow during this period.

It might be better to place it in a pot, water the root area as soon as you can and then on a daily basis thereafter. Don't water the leaves, for they will attract the sun and this might make them act like a magnifying glass, in which case the sun could easily burn small holes through them.

During the autumn period, deciduous trees lose their leaves and become dormant until the following spring. This is quite natural. A little later into the season is a good time to plant a tree, for this gives it plenty of time to settle in prior to the winter period.

Ideally, winter is about the best time to plant most trees because the majority of the many varieties tend to sleep then. This means that placing your new tree in a new home will not upset any natural balance. Always remember that it is unwise to plant a tree during icy weather. So, at such a time, do make sure that you protect the roots from frost until you can place it where you wish.

CITRUS TREES

Of course, there are always a few variations on a theme when it comes to trees. For example, a citrus tree is an outside plant that has to have a lot of extra help to protect it against frost. These plants give year-round pleasure with their fragrant flowering buds as they gradually grow into their fruiting period. So, during the spring and as the weather gradually becomes warmer, sunnier and brighter, you will need to take extra special care because temperatures in sun-rooms or in conservatories and greenhouses can soar.

As the frost decreases and spring begins to wear on, temperatures will rise. Now is a good time to move the tree outside. Toward the end of May or the beginning of June is a good time but much will, and does, depend on our (English) weather. It is best to site the tree in a shady spot at this time. After a week or so it can be moved into a full sun position for the rest of the summer. Citrus trees love sunny weather, so the more the merrier. However, should you want to keep one indoors then make sure it is near a window in a cool room.

As and when the autumn period begins to settle in, you may move any outside plant back indoors, preferably before it begins to get too chilly or windy, which is usually around the end of October and the beginning of November.

Before the winter period really takes hold, either bring citrus trees indoors or keep them in a reasonably warm greenhouse. They need plenty of light and will do well if near or by a south-facing window. Try to maintain a continuous temperature, somewhere between 4°–15°C. Any sudden changes are quite unhelpful to these rather sensitive plants.

Don't put any of these trees in water for any reason. If it appears to have dried up then gently water the compost, which may well have to be every day in sunny summer weather and then about every two or three weeks in the winter. Keep the watering can in the same room so that the temperature will be kept even. Also, it doesn't hurt to add a citrus feed to these watering times. As a rule, the trees tend to keep their shape so that pruning, if any, may be kept to an absolute minimum. A snip here and there should be all that is needed at any time.

FRUIT TREES

For several reasons, each of the various fruit trees are quite different. What most people don't realise is that no fruit tree is native to this country. They all come from abroad. It never fails to amuse me when I see or hear a local puff him-, or herself, up all proud, pontificating about their apple, pear or plum trees and how well they have done. The apple tree originated in Kazakhstan, while the pear tree and the cherry came from China or Vietnam.

The plum tree we now know came originally from Iran, while the damson tree came from Damascus and, latterly, from Italy – where it really is quite cherished. As expected, the orange tree has its roots in the east, mostly India, with the lemon tree being found originally in north-east India and parts of China. Curiously, the grapefruit tree has its origins in Barbados.

Because of these rather warm areas, perhaps one can now appreciate that their roots should (must) be kept dry and away from any sudden temperature change in any season. Pruning is best carried out by removing unnecessary branch growth, leaves or stem extensions during the winter period. These essentially garden trees almost always need protection against frost.

Once spring has arrived, they really will all flourish in any sunny position preferably close to a fence, hedge or wall that helps to protect against wind or sudden temperature changes. They usually blossom in the spring and almost certainly will be pollinated by birds or the local bee population, unless it is a self-pollinating growth like an apple or a pear tree.

In the summer, all of these fruit plants positively adore the sun and need a lot to help ripen their fruits. So, to get the best results, always keep your fruit tree in a sheltered position but where it also receives a lot of sunshine. Some trees will need protection from some of the garden birds or they will take the small fruit as the blossom falls away. A simple small squared netting usually does this trick quite well.

During the autumn is the best time for most fruit trees because of their offering. As fruit ripens and is picked or drops away to the ground, gather it all in and store in a cool but airy place. As a rule, you should try to water fruit trees daily during sunny summer weather. It will also be helpful to them if you could find the time to ensure they are well fed.

Nutrients for their energy to grow and remain healthy should be given at least once a month during the summer, preferably with an organic fertiliser. They don't need pruning that often but their branches will almost always be looking for more space in which to grow. A simple snip from the ends of these little growths should be enough to encourage new branches that tend to lay further back and help to create a nice bushy tree in good general condition.

Pruning is best carried out during the winter, in December or January.

ORNAMENTAL TREES

As long as you remember to water the soil more or less each day during hot and dry periods and keep the roots well drained, they will seem to go on forever. Also remember that as these plants live out in the open all the time, they will need protection against frost.

In the spring, as the weather becomes sunny and brighter, it is important to make sure that these types of growths are allowed to stay in sunny positions near to a fence, hedge or wall, to help protect them from the wind and frost.

As the summer wears on and gradually disposes of the dangers of a frost, it is acceptable to move them to a good position until the summer gives way to the more autumnal weather, to work its way in. Then, if need be, by all means, move them again to where you consider the best place might be in your particular garden. Try not to over water, because this can be quite harmful. Once a day will suffice in hot summery weather, but once or twice a week should be enough otherwise.

Try to keep an eye open for the first frosts of autumn, or until your local weather really begins to have a chill in it. Put the tree where you think best, preferably back up against the protection of a fence, hedge or wall. This will probably be toward the end of October. It won't hurt to keep your ornamental trees in the same full sun position and south-facing during the winter period.

These plants are evergreens and must have a lot of light during winter, especially if there are strong winds with which they may have to contend. To keep them looking good all year round, it doesn't hurt to re-pot them about six months or so after acquiring them. Their roots need to be kept clean and free from possible infection, and this exercise will ensure that they will remain healthy. When you re-site them, you can check them much more closely to see what, if anything, might be needed. Pots should have good, clear open holes for drainage. A layer of stones at their base will help. Fill the pot with fresh clean top soil.

Should any of these plants need pruning, snip with a good pair of secateurs when branches or leaves start to get out of hand. Pruning should be carried out little and often and is better done in the spring or early summer months, but only if it is needed.

ROSES

It is imperative that any new rose you buy or are given is removed from its wrapping as soon as possible. Work in some water, not too much, to its new container or hole in the ground. Plant the growth reasonably quickly, after which you should add a little water each morning to the root area in dry weather. As this is a deciduous plant, you won't get to see too much in the way of change until the early spring, when buds will start to appear. In good, bright, fairly warm weather, this can often happen earlier than you expect.

A lot of care and attention will be needed if planting out in the summer. The roots (never the leaves) must be watered regularly. Also, remember to 'dead-head' (take away dead, dying or superfluous flower heads), for this encourages growth. While you are at it, be on the look-out for the variety of summer pests and treat them according to what they are.

As autumn closes in, these plants will start to lose their leaves and, as they go, so do the flowers die off, leaving a pretty awful looking plain remainder. This is just about the best time to plant fresh roses and also to carry out pruning exercises. While the book might say this ought to be carried out during September or October, a little later won't hurt.

Any stems and or unwanted branches should be cut back to any point you wish, but if there are any buds showing or if there is a fork in the wood, trim just in front of this. Clear away the debris, which will help to avoid the possibility of disease. Leave until late spring or early summer, when you ought to appraise how things are going then.

CHRISTMAS TREES

To ensure your indoor tree remains in good condition and does not readily drop its needles, a fir Christmas tree should be cut down just prior to the 11th full Moon of the local calendar year, which is usually in November (in 2022, this will be in Sagittarius, on the 23rd). Just occasionally, it can sometimes occur in December. Always remember that spruce trees do tend to lose their needles earlier than the fir.

PLANTING TREES

Most fruit trees should be planted when the Moon is in Taurus or Libra, although the apple should be planted when the Moon is in Sagittarius. You will see from the attached list that quince trees should be put in during the first or second quarter, when the Moon is in Capricorn.

From an astrological point of view, we tend to look at trees in general as 'perennials' and much prefer to use the

PLANT	PHASE	SIGN
Annuals	1 or 2	Libra
Apple tree	3	Taurus, Cancer, Sagittarius, Pisces
Apricot tree	2 or 3	Taurus, Libra, Capricorn
Ash tree	2 or 3	Venus, Jupiter
Beech tree	2 or 3	Capricorn
Cherry tree	2 or 3	Taurus, Libra, Capricorn
Damson	2 or 3	Sagittarius
Deciduous tree	2 or 3	Cancer, Virgo, Libra, Scorpio, Pisces
Evergreen tree	2 or 3	Cancer, Virgo, Libra, Scorpio, Pisces
Fig tree	2 or 3	Taurus, Libra
Grapefruit	2 or 3	Sagittarius
Horse chestnut	2 or 3	Taurus
Lemon	2 or 3	Sagittarius
Maple tree	2 or 3	Taurus, Cancer, Virgo, Pisces
Nectarine tree	2 or 3	Taurus, Virgo, Libra
Nut tree	2 or 3	Cancer, Scorpio, Pisces
Oak tree	3	Sagittarius
Orange	2 or 3	Sagittarius
Peach tree	2 or 3	Taurus, Virgo, Libra
Pear tree	2 or3	Taurus, Virgo, Libra
Plum tree	2 or 3	Taurus, Virgo, Libra
Quince	1 or 2	Capricorn
Tree (shade)	3	Taurus, Capricorn
Tree (ornamental)	2	Taurus, Libra

third quarter Moon for planting. This is probably more for astrological technical reasons than actual gardening ideas.

When a plant is put in during a decreasing Moon, it helps create a better root formation and the slower growth of the top of the tree becomes better protected. Trees in general that are planted at this time will often have a slightly thicker bark and almost always have a longer life.

PRUNING TREES

For the best results, one should prune a tree only when the Moon is waning and passing through Aries, Leo or Sagittarius. Equally, but with not quite as good an effect, you can also carry out this exercise when the Moon is on the wane, during either Gemini or Sagittarius.

The best planting times for the various bushes, shrubs and trees are listed on previous page.

Trees and Religion

Throughout the ages, trees have been said to have been used in religious practices. A tree was often regarded as being a home to a tree spirit. In some European writings going back centuries, there seems to have always been a heavy involvement in these kinds of practices. Many of these took place in what became sacred groves, especially where the oak was involved.

A tree was often used to symbolise a god or other sacred being, or it could have stood for what was then considered sacred in general. Some trees were thought to have represented a certain deity or even an ancestor. It was also thought of as a mediator or as a link to that religious ideal and was associated with the then beliefs in a heaven or an afterlife of some kind.

This sort of thinking was almost certainly one of the most ancient forms of religious belief in those far off days. In some European areas, there are remnants of an extremely wide variety of this kind of belief to be found. In Uppsala in Sweden, and in areas of Lithuania and Rome there is much evidence of this reverence or worship of trees. What evidence that has been left behind suggests that groves or special sites were created to play their role in this most important spiritual role, in the then religious thinking.

The Hindu worship of trees was, for quite different thinking, featured in their mythology. It might have been for the then thinking of immortality, fertility or for fulfilling wishes. They all connected in some way to the many various rituals performed with the utmost of spiritual ideals. The banyan tree was and still is revered in parts of India and other places in the Middle and Far East.

Like the European yew, the banyan also sends shoots down from its low-lying branches and, when they reach the ground, they develop a rooting ability. Another unusual ability of this growth is that even when all else may be still, the slightest air movement will stir its leaves. This tree has, therefore, created special beliefs in the minds of those who still meet or shelter beneath its branches. It is also worth remembering that the banyan is used for its several medicinal properties.

The old religious tree-based centres were all much of a muchness, in that they may have differed here and there, but only slightly. The most ancient grove at Uppsala in Sweden is clearly linked-in with the Norse mythology of old. In Uppsala there was, apparently, a triple throne in the centre of which the 'greatest god', Thor, is alleged to have sat in order to rule. On either side of him would have been Wodan or Odin, as we now know him, and Fricco or Freyr.

Close by this central point is a large woodland preserve of ancient trees upon which many males or rarely (if ever) females, were offered up for sacrifice. It was revered by the locals, many of whom would have been 'heathen' tribes. They were so-called largely because of the many sacrificial deaths that they carried out.

A huge remainder grove was also found at the same point, where the gods of these trees would have been worshipped. In the centre of them all was an enormous evergreen tree with a lightly moving spring nearby. Stories report that the whole site was destroyed sometime before the end of the eleventh century by King Inge the Elder.

As we come further forward in history, we note that much religious feeling became centred toward the world of trees. The huge giants that seemed to reign supreme over the smaller growths there appeared (to the people) to offer their allegiance in the way that they grew, that is, not as strongly. There were and still are quite a variety of stories relating to the worship of the ash, oak and yew trees, among others. It has always been thought that many people in those far off times felt it almost obligatory to find a religious symbol that everyone could recognise and accept.

The world of the ever and always growing tree attracted them and their beliefs. Trees had links with many events that occurred in the past. To them, their logic also linked trees with the present that would also be there in the future for those yet to come. The yew tree played an important role here. Large sites of them were created where they did not already exist, to be become recognised as symbolic of death and rebirth by many.

The land they used for these groves became hallowed in their eyes. That, and that a yew can seem to live for a thousand years or more, and that it is also an evergreen, meant much to these folk. Low growing branches are known to create fresh roots on them and these new growths seek fresh food and water to assist its long life. This life and spirit of the yew tree has always been an attraction for religious fervour.

Tree worship was and still is practiced in New Zealand, where the great Pohutukawa tree on the North Island still grows ever strong today. On Cape Reinga, right at the top of the island is, perhaps, the most sacred place for any of the indigenous Maori people. Many believe this is where many of those who have gone before began their final journey to the spirit world. Much of the area is now protected as sacred land, where people seem to come from anywhere to plant a tree in the remembrance of a loved one.

It is now accepted that the Pohutukawa is a much-favoured tree, even for the practising Christian fraternity. It features strongly, rather like a national Christmas tree. In December, as pictured on cards, and during the Kiwi celebrations, the tree grows red blooms, as if perpetuating its hold on all and sundry, whether they are tree worshippers or otherwise.

Many hundreds of years ago, tree worship was rife in many places in Japan and had several different guises. There was no direct opposition to each, either then or today. They all had their own beliefs and ideals. Many trees in Japan, such as the pine tree (of which there are many) are named 'Mastu'. The best translation for this would be, "waiting for a god's soul to come down from heaven ..."

Elsewhere, in the south of the country, there is the Ogatama-noki tree, which means, "inviting a soul." People believed in this so strongly that they ensured at least one of them was planted near to or at the entrance of a holy grove or shrine that they created for such an event.

Historically, there are about a dozen or more special shrines connected in some way with Japanese Buddhism, or the Shinto faith. It has become customary to plant pine and/or bamboo trees at the sites and to place small collections of pine twigs by the gates of houses each New Year to ensure, hopefully, a blessing from one of the gods.

One of these shrines was created by the government in the 1920's to remember the Meiji Emperor. People from all over the country partook in some way, either by the giving of their time or of trees to place in the grove.

It has now grown into a wonderful forest of special broad-leaved trees, along with the Hinoki tree. Where wood has been needed for special construction work, the Hinoki tree has been used. The ideal of these special memorial purposes seems to have spread in these modern times to many parts of the UK but not quite for the same reasons.

So many families today are unable to pay the high cost of funerals for departed loved ones. To get around this, many people are putting the pots of the ashes of loved ones into the local church yard, other quiet places, or in their gardens.

They are also planting small trees by them in order to commemorate the lives of these past souls. This is helping to increase the growth of trees in this country, which has cut down far more of them than we have ever planted and for which we are now paying quite dearly in so many ways.

It would be quite wrong to leave these tree-worshipping groups, that once were or still are extant in our modern-day world, without mentioning the Druids. The Druid adores and venerates the tree in all its ways. They will often pay a visit to one particular tree in a shrine or a grove they have created in a wood or forest to meditate or simply commune with nature in their own way.

The main Druid Order supports the work of organising sacred grove planting to help their own followers or the general public woodland sanctuaries where they may safely pursue their own beliefs. The word "Druid" is derived from the old English word for oak and the Indo-European root 'wid'. Together, this has been acknowledged to mean "a person at one with the knowledge of the oak." Over the years, this has come to be taken as "one with knowledge of the tree" or "a wood or forest sage."

Those who train as Druids are taught to learn the way of the trees. They are taught that one can obtain certain medicines from this or that tree, or that others have various gifts that man can use, once he knows how.

The male Druid supports women in their world at all levels and has done so for many years. In this order, there has almost always been a place for an equal number of women and men within its leadership and the lower roles. Perhaps the most well-known female Druid today is Emma Restall Orr.

It is rather nice to see that women were more than well looked after in paganism, far more than they were ever tolerated or respected in the accepted church systems of old or those of the present day. In the world of the heathen, with famous female names such as Galina Grasskova and Diana Paxon, there are many others who take part in all manner of pagan beliefs and traditions. They stand along with the men in equal roles of leadership and teaching.

Historically, we have always known that there were female Druids, more often referred to as 'Druidesses'. The Greeks and Romans were extremely interested in these old Celtic ideals that were so very alien to their own ways. This was especially so when it came to positions of leadership and the powers that women held.

Because of the way that women were regarded in their normal society, we have only the slightest snippets of information in respect of their role in Druidry. They rarely refer to women in their accounts of the old Celtic societies, no matter who was making these records.

In these modern times, we learn that those who prefer to study Druidry are taught how to work with the power of old Mother Nature. They study by using the Ogham. This is a most ancient form of a written language, whose origins are quite lost in the mists of time. It has a lot of similarities with the Nordic runes but is totally different in many other respects. Today, the Ogham is said to be the main manner of communication between the Druids and is regarded as the alphabet of their knowledge of tree lore.

There are many Druid groves and shrines dotted about all over the English countryside. Some have been only recently created, while many others have been in situ for centuries. There are equally as many in Ireland, Scotland, Wales and especially Cornwall. They are all of different ages and sizes but all dedicated by and to the Druids who still use them today.

There are also many other sites or just places in woods or forests where Druids will visit to either meditate or commune with nature as they see fit. Most of them assist the work of the three main tree-planting charities. In addition, they make a point of supporting any public efforts in this direction, as well as teaching their own members how and where to create the best place for a shrine that can be used over and over again.

Lure and Lore

THE APPLE

The apple tree appears in prehistoric times as the common or wild apple and was native to Europe and western Asia. Remains of sliced apples on plates and saucers were seen in tombs that have been dated to well over 5,000 years-old. The Greeks and Romans were known to have grown apple trees during their periods of influence. The healing properties of the apple were known and used by many of the ancients who were involved in their respective workings where the tree was grown.

There were, apparently, over 20 varieties of the fruit in ancient times while today it is thought there may be as many as 2,000 or even more. The only really domestic apple to England is the crab apple which has some similarities to the cider apple. This tree is a part of the rose family that are known to include the magical Ogham trees such as the rowan, hawthorn and blackthorn as well as the cherry, plum and pear trees. As a matter of passing interest the crab apple is the plant badge of Scotland's Clan Lamont, part of whose territories were known to have been around the Argyll area.

THE ASH

There are a huge number of trees in England, many of which are variations on the principal, as we know them.

An example of this is the ash tree, of which there are as many as 50 or more different varieties all over the world. In England, there are around ten or more, with the white ash being the largest of them all. History has shown that the ash tree is related to the olive tree.

The leaves of some ash tree species may turn purple, red or yellow in colour, usually in the autumn, and all bear clusters of winged seeds. The black and green ash trees may reach as high as 18m, although the black ash seems to prefer the colder areas, where it survives quite happily.

This tree is highly regarded in many places, perhaps more so in Celtic writings and especially with the Welsh. In Wales, one of the many ancient gods, Gwyddon, was said to use a wand or staff of ash when he was healing and in matters of enchantment. The ash was frequently employed in creating the shafts of spears and handles for other weaponry. The name of the ash is said to come from the old Anglo-Saxon name of 'asec', which was a word that meant "ritual spear".

THE BEECH

Beech tree groves are usually found to have been created near places of power, such as Avebury or Cerne Abbas. These old sites were often used for food as well as for their stirring appearance. Some claim the beech may have created the ideas for constructing cathedrals.

It is often claimed that the beech is considered to be the mother of the woods, where it may also be called the 'Beech Queen' who is said to have the Royal Oak as its consort. The beech is held in high regard as a generous growth, for she supplies both food and protection when she opens and fans her broad branches. So many creatures benefit from the shelter, and her 'fruit' – her beech nuts – are a wonderful food source. Many local people used to rely on her nuts to help get themselves through moments of major hunger, when proper food was in short supply or non-existent, something that often happened in the old days.

The nuts were collected, saved and used to supplement what scarce food they may have had at the time. It is said that this helped to strengthen the bond between the various communities. Beech was also used as a good luck charm. Some pieces were thought to bring good fortune to those who wore them.

BIRCH

Chiefly known as the White Lady of the Woods, as well as the white birch, this tree has a rather graceful growth, with long branches that always seem to be reaching upward to the sky. It rarely grows on its own and is more than likely to be found in a grove or a shrine. Recognised more as a 'she', this plant always appears as a rather graceful feminine affair. The birch often appears to grow from out of a common or otherwise joined trunk. Those who say that they have been 'claimed' by the birch often appear as rather gentle people themselves.

Not many realise just how useful the birch can be, for it supplies a lot of cover for quite an array of flying bird life, as well as providing nesting space and food for many of other animals. The deer and hare will nibble and eat the leaves or the smaller saplings of birch. The mature tree provides plenty of cover for a wealth of animals. Beavers and porcupines will eat the bark, along with shrews and voles that prefer to make the most of the available buds and seeds.

THE BLACKTHORN

This is a deciduous tree. The leaves turn yellow in the autumn and, eventually, they all fall off in the early winter days to leave a rather ugly looking black type of growth just 'sitting' there until the spring comes again.

Strictly speaking, the blackthorn is more like a large shrub, not a tree and, as such, I was reluctant to include it. Tradition implies that the plant only grows to about 3–4m in height. However, it does seem to appear all over the British Isles, mostly on the edge of woodlands, as a rule. Its bark is scaly but do take care because it is covered in rather dreadful long, sharp thorns. If they pierce your skin, you will receive the most painful wounds that can easily turn septic.

It does, however, have some good uses. The sloe berry is often used to make ink or a red dye. Elsewhere, country folk use the wood to make walking sticks, while in other areas the berries are gathered in to make sloe gin and/or fruit jam. It is also noted for some of its medicinal uses.

THE ELDER

The elder is a smallish tree, usually absolutely covered with rather colourful blossoms during the summer and then in the autumn it produces lovely juicy berries that country people use in making jam, jellies, medicinal drinks and various wines. It has many hollow branches that are helpful for creating all sorts of bellows and pipes. The name, elder, is probably associated with the Anglo-Saxon word 'eller', which means "a kindler of fire." In Ireland, for many a year the elder was regarded as a sacred tree and it was seriously frowned upon to use any part of it, even a fallen branch or twig.

In the Ogham calendar, which gives a letter and a tree to each month, the elder is the tree of the thirteenth month and is called 'Ruis' to signify the letter R. The tree carries a message of change, transformation and spiritual renewal.

This particular growth bears much ill repute from its alleged use as the cross on which Christ was crucified and then as the tree that Judas Iscariot later hanged himself. Because of this, it has been called the 'emblem of death'. This unhelpful name is actually much older and predates Christianity quite a bit.

THE ELM

The elm has strong connections with the Underworld as well as a special relationship with the world of the elf. The elm can be among some of the largest of our native trees. As with the oak, it had many folklore stories associated with it, some involving other trees. Among these were the elms on Humberside or those in Devon, around which May Day festivities were held.

Because of their size, their use in hedges often made them landmarks or boundary points. Judges would often hold court beneath them and preachers were known to preach their messages as well. The elm bends and distorts its shape easily. The 'wych' elm bears out the wood being pliant, but not to witches who wouldn't touch it because it was thought the wood was unsuitable as a burning fuel.

Despite these problems, the elm can be and is used for building boats and/or barges, bridges and wagon wheels. The elm was once used to make water pipes before metal ones came in. Ancient archers would make longbows from the elm and coffins are still made from it too.

In Scotland, it was used for dyeing wool while some folk used the elm in some medical matters. Many people were known to chew or boil the inner bark because when cooked in this fashion the bark was most effective for treating burn areas.

THE FURZE

The furze sets the spring alight with a dazzling display of bright yellow flowers following on from the usually drab days of winter. It is one of the first flowering spring plants often in full flow before April is out and the bees love it. Also known as gorse it is an evergreen and is a part of the pea family. It has small leaves that latterly create a long needle type thorn shape. Furze is an Anglo-Saxon word that translates as gorse from "gorst" that means "waste". The plant loves the open moorland.

Furze is used by gardeners for many purposes, mostly to keep wild life from what they are cultivating and it is used as a covering material for game birds. Bakers were known to use it to fuel their ovens. The ashes may be mixed in with animal fats to produce a soap substitute. It was spread on fields to help the soil and is still used as an animal food because it is said that it has half the protein value of oats.

Both bark and flowers create a yellow dye. The flowers give colour and flavour to beer and whisky. The flowers are also used to help make tea and wine. The furze tree buds also help to create white wine vinegar and a salt solution for pickle.

THE HAWTHORN

The hawthorn used to be called the 'May'. This accounts for why it is ever linked with the month, especially in many parts of England. It is alleged the knights and ladies of old would ride out on the first morning of the month. This term does not refer to the month of May, but to the flowering hawthorns that they would gather in to decorate their halls and rooms.

When we read the old-style calendar that was in use until we changed it in the eighteenth century, the woods would have been bright and glorious with the May and other blossoms. There were many other old customs followed to welcome in summer in many rural areas until quite recently. In some villages, locals would band together and leave a branch of hawthorn at each house whilst singing traditional songs.

May was the month for courting and other similar activities after the winter was well and truly over and might account for why the hawthorn is so often found linked with all the merry-making. In ancient Greece, the hawthorn (May) was used for marriage ceremonies. In many areas, young girls used to (and still do) wear crowns of hawthorn.

THE HAZEL

The hazel tree and wisdom have been linked for centuries. Sacred to Thor in Norse culture, it was also recognised by the Romans, who associated it with Mercury, who was known for his intelligence.

The English word 'hazel' comes down to us from the Anglo-Saxon 'haesl', which meant "the baton of authority." The Celts also associated the hazel with inspiration and wisdom the Gaelic word 'cnocach'. The Gaelic word for hazel is 'coll' and this is seen in place names in Scotland, like the Isle of Coll, for example. It is also a part of the name of Clan Colquhoun whose badge is the hazel. It sometimes grows as a clump of trunks but it tends to use just one trunk and a canopy shape that works quite well, particularly after coppicing. The wood is very durable and has been used to make staffs for Druidic ritual purposes and was often used for medieval weapons; particularly arrow shafts, as the branches tend to grow very straight and don't warp as much as other types of wood.

Pilgrims used it as a staff, while shepherds made crooks and walking sticks from it. Water diviners use hazel fork twigs to find water and other things, while the leaves make a reasonable food when fed to cattle. Some say the leaf can help to increase a cow's milk yield. Hazelnuts helped to provide protein and were often ground and mixed with flour to be made into bread.

THE HOLLY

Holly trees grow to around 3–4m high and are famous for their spiky leaves. The trunk is grey but becomes quite gnarled as it grows older. Like the beech, it is one of our few native trees that prefer the shade. Only the female tree produces the bright red berries. Both trees are pollinated by birds and insects, which is why they appear in gardens when there is no other tree nearby.

The wood burns very well and may be used for carving. In olden days, it was grown as fodder for cattle and deer in the winter. It was favoured to grow in hedgerows because it is hardy and act as a barrier for stock all year. The tree was once used in pagan rites on Shrove Tuesday festivals. Holly in the house at Christmas links with the re-birth of the sun at the winter solstice. It is interesting to note that the original Yule log burned at Christmas was the holly.

Some place names in old English history might have been where the tree originally grew. Among them were Holm or Hollin, Hollins Green, Hollinfare and Holmesdale in Surrey. Blackbirds, fieldfares and thrushes all eat holly berries and spread the seeds. Many nest in the tree because its leaves offer them protection when they roost in the winter.

THE IVY

The ivy (or Hedera) is one of some ten or so varieties of climbing or ground-based evergreen plants found in many areas. It grows in Europe, north-west Africa, Asia and Japan. It can grow on trees and rock faces and is known to climb to some 25–30m above ground level. There are two leaf types. The sharp pointed version usually found on the climbing stems, and the plain leaf variety found on the flowers high in the trees. The local wildlife, bees, birds and other insects regard the fruit and flowers as important food sources.

The fruit is a small black berry that ripens during the winter but it quite poisonous to humans. The ivy was sacred to Osiris in Greek mythology, along with Dionysus. In Roman mythology, it has become associated with the god of wine, Bacchus, because it grew all over his home. The god is often pictured wearing a crown of ivy, perhaps because it was thought to prevent intoxication. In Europe, it is often grown up around the outside of a house to act as a protector. It is often carried by brides.

THE OAK

The oak is England's national tree and is the top dog as far as we are concerned. Famous for its longevity and strength, we know it as the pride and glory of any wood or forest. Also regarded as the holy tree of Europe, it was sacred to Zeus and Jupiter and was recognised as the tree of the Thunder God, Thor.

Its name comes down to us from the Greek word 'drus', that some feel is also the origin of the term 'Druid'. As the druids have always been very closely linked with groves and forests, it is not surprising to find it held sacred by people who lived among the oaks. They also used the wood to build parts of their dwellings, to provide fuel for burning, and the acorns for food.

Combined with the word 'wid' (to know), the word for Druid may have referred to those who were gifted with a special knowledge of the oak, known also as the 'wise ones of the wood.' There are some who think that the tree could be an entry into the nether world itself.

THE ROWAN

The rowan is deciduous, small and prefers high ground, although these days it grows in lowland areas quite happily. At first, one might think it looks like an ash but it is actually a part of the rose, hawthorn, blackthorn and cherry group. It is known to live for up to 200 years and can grow up to about 12m. It blossoms in May with small white flowers, has small leaves in pairs and bright red berries in the autumn that birds adore.

The berry is also used in different Celtic areas. The Scots make wine with it while the Irish prefer to use it to flavour mead. The Welsh brew beer with it. Rowan berry jelly is still eaten with game in Scotland. The tree also has a variety of names, the most well-known of which is the mountain ash. The rowan also appears as a part of the clan badge of the Malcolms and McLachlans.

Rowan wood is strong, makes good walking sticks and is used for carving. Druids were known to use the bark and berries to dye material worn during various ceremonies. The bark was also used in tanning processes, while some used its twigs to divine items, especially metal. In England, the tree has a long history as a growth to protect against witchcraft.

THE SPINDLE

The spindle's colourful wood is used to make spindles and, in some places, toothpicks were a most practical idea. It once made a medicine for a range of various ills until it was found to have a digitalis-like effect. In flower from May to June; the seeds ripen from September to November. The flowers are pollinated by insects. More of a shrub than a tree, it is found in hedgerows as a smooth-leaved shrub.

Its abundant fruit usually comes in threes and is not unlike a red rose colour that bursts open when ripe. It makes an excellent yellow dye when boiled in water, but also a green one when alum is added. The berries are harmful to young humans and fatal to some animals, especially sheep. Many years ago, it was used by herbalists who called it skewer-wood. With a light-yellow hue, the wood is strong and used to make pipe-stems in a few European areas. It is helpful with a role in the manufacture of gunpowder. Probably because the wood is so easy to work, it may be found in a wide variety of domestic furniture items.

THE SYCAMORE

It was brought to England some six or seven hundred years ago, probably by the Romans; while others think it might have been the Crusaders because they were known to bring home all manner of new things, such as the sycamore, because they considered it was sacred. They brought it back from Egypt. It was thought that Mary and Jesus stopped to rest under its spreading branches on their flight into Egypt. It is also suggested they might have used it when creating the original building of the Temple of Solomon.

On Mount Lothian, when William Wallace was knighted, it is claimed that sycamores were planted to commemorate the event. People who love trees believe that when a tree is brought in from elsewhere and then reproduces, they can then claim it as a native growth. The sycamore has helped many people to survive the wet, windswept Western Islands. These great trees have stood for over 150 years and are a reminder of what a majestic growth a tree can be.

Workers use the wood for many things, but it is especially good for making musical instruments and even butcher's blocks. It is thought that a seven acre set of trees will not only self-replenish but will supply enough shelter and fuel for one family for life.

THE WILLOW

This is most often located near or by water and has a long association of being most rewarding and useful for magical and medical matters. It is also useful in other areas such as honey production and for keeping bees happy. Often called the 'weeping willow', it is not the tree used in the Ogham. Not many realise that there are around some 300 variations or species of the willow tree.

It is agreed that it is closely related to the poplar. In North America, there are about 30 native or natural tree families, along with at least double that in shrub-like form. In the Ogham, the willow also represents the Monday tree, the letter s and the number 5. It has been used as the symbol of the Ovate grade of Druidry.

Wildlife associations are mainly the hawk and thrush from the world of birds. From animal life are the hare and the cat, while the herbs are mostly the mistletoe and the primrose. It is one of the Seven Sacred Irish Trees as well as a sacred Druid tree. When you knock on a willow tree, it is said to refute bad luck and is alleged to be the origin of the superstitious expression 'touch wood' or 'knock on wood.'

THE YEW

It was once thought that the dark and beautiful yew was the only evergreen in England. Druids, who believed in re-incarnation; and then the Christians, with their ideas on resurrection, looked upon it as the natural symbolism in respect of everlasting life. The Irish once thought this and many still do. The yew has a reputation for long life, which is probably because of the unusual way in which it usually grows.

Many of its branches grow down, form shoots and enter the ground to create new stems. These eventually grow up around the old growth as a separate but linked trunk. After a while it becomes almost impossible to tell the new from the old or original growth. Thus, the yew has symbolised death and re-birth in its own way for centuries; or the young that springs from the old – a fitting study for all at the beginning of any new year.

Magic and Superstition

THE APPLE

It is considered to be unlucky to completely take all the apples from the tree. One should always leave two or three for the birds. Another suggestion is that a few more should be left for the fairies. On the night of a full or new Moon, if a young unmarried girl should sit in front of her mirror at midnight and eat an apple, on the last bite an image of her future partner might be seen looking over her shoulder.

Stop men from arguing by cutting into the skin of an apple and then throwing it between them. This was believed to stop an argument and then to settle the issue more peacefully. Never destroy an apple tree or you will have bad luck for a long time to come.

THE ASH

The ash tree is alleged to safeguard and protect all who live a house when the flowers, leaves, branches or larger chunks of the wood are hung inside or outside. Many of the older superstitions were probably created because it was a long-held belief that the tree had strong associations with the Ash Wednesday celebrations. That, and also a very old suggestion from Devon, which says that when the Infant Jesus was given his first bath, it was heated by a fire of ash wood. In many areas of the old English countryside, children were asked bring a small twig of ash to school on the day. Anyone who forgot this had his or her feet jumped on by the children who had remembered to bring it.

THE BEECH

There is practically nothing to worry about, with the exception that no-one, especially pregnant women, should eat cooked beech nuts or serious stomach problems will be likely. Because it is thought that a beech tree has never been reported for being struck by lightning during a heavy rain storm, people used to look for and run to a beech tree for safety. Their superstition that lightning does not or will not strike the beech tree is incorrect. As a matter of fact, it does get hit but the tree is constructed in such a way that the strike's power is somehow neutralised by the tree. Curiously, even today, everybody agrees it is probably the best tree under which to shelter at such times.

THE BIRCH

Cradles made from birch wood were believed to protect new-born babies, and, in Scottish folklore it is thought that when a pregnant cow is herded with a birch wood stick, she will have healthy offspring. If she should not be pregnant at that time, she would soon become so. Thus, the birch is seen by some to have magical pioneering power. This may later have been one of the reasons the birch has been used in the 'Beating the Bounds' rituals in many areas, or why many gardeners use birch besoms (brooms) to clean their gardens. Besoms are believed to be witches' broomsticks. One very strong superstition in some country areas is to decorate a birch tree and fix it to a stable door on May Day to protect the horses inside.

THE BLACKTHORN

The blackthorn is used a lot as a boundary growth marker in hedges but it also has something of a superstitious reputation and in many ancient tree legends it is associated with bad luck.

Known as the 'Mother of the Woods,' in some places it is seen as both a bad and a good luck omen, depending on where you live or work. There is a lot to think about here because it is traditionally said to be the collection of bushes and trees that protected the Sleeping Beauty Princess. Then it is also thought to be because the wand of a witch is made from the blackthorn.

However you view it, farmers still prefer to use its spiny branches and twigs to provide the natural barriers to keep all their livestock secure.

THE ELDER

In western parts of Europe, it is still said to be unlucky to use elder branches indoors. Curiously, and often within the same area, it is also believed to protect against witchcraft. Traditions do vary, for some say the tree must not be cut down because the "elder be ye lady's tree, burn it not or cursed ye will be." However, in other places the tree could only be cut down safely if you chanted verse to the Elder Mother.

To sleep under the elder will give you quite vivid dreams of fairies. This, despite witches were thought to be able to turn into an elder tree for the night. Each one is thought to be inhabited by an Elder Mother. In some Scandinavian areas, one must not use a cradle made of elder wood or the child would suffer "one way or another".

THE ELM

It was long thought that the elm tree was a tree of treachery. It was thought to be quite averse to humans and usually grew near or by passes and paths that were believed to lead out of this mortal world.

It was said to be one of the stories of Orpheus who, when he rescued Eurydice from the Underworld, bemused all around by playing music on his harp. It is alleged that when he stopped, the first Elm grove sprang up.

Elm trees began to grow so widespread in hedges and elsewhere that people began to think they were lucky for all to use. It was believed that one always had a fair hearing from judges who held court under their shade.

The term 'wych' in wych elm meant that the wood bent easily and did not refer to witches. As a result, it became lucky to use the wood in building work. It was also thought to be lucky to be buried in a coffin made from elm wood.

THE FURZE

More of a bush than a tree, the furze usually grows quite widespread in hedgerows. It can be used in domestic areas because the very sharp spines of this bush help to create a first-class barrier for containing livestock. It is said to grow like wild fire, thus making it a tad too hard to want to handle by some farmers. Before any restrictions were imposed in respect of unlicensed burning, old growths were disposed of in this fashion to aid the nourishment of the soil. The ashes of a burned furze are alkaline, which makes them perfect for fertilising.

The furze tree and bush involve both magic along with good and bad luck. It was thought that if you cut, trim or damage one then you will have bad luck for long periods. It is also thought that delays to road works were caused because the tree was cut down without knowing what it was. Those who did know would refuse to cut it or touch it. It is considered to be good luck if given a furze bush, for the flowers are thought to be symbolic of the spring equinox. The tree is also thought of as a symbol of fertility and protects against evil.

THE HAWTHORN

It is said to be bad luck to cut down or attempt to trim a hawthorn tree that stands alone. In these modern times, farmers still tend to work around them. It was thought, and still is in some areas in England, that Jesus created the Holy Grail from the hawthorn. This is the goblet He used at the Last Supper. Joseph of Arimathea, who was related to Jesus, supposedly took Him along on one of his many trading journeys and they visited the legendary Isle of Avalon.

At the crucifixion, Joseph collected some of the Lord's blood in the same goblet. When he got back to England he is alleged to have pushed his staff into the Wearyall Hill. The staff rooted and became the hawthorn known as the Glastonbury Thorn. Many people of those olden days took this as a sign that Christianity would do well here. Later, Joseph was alleged to have built the first Christian church in this country, at Glastonbury. He then hid the Grail somewhere locally and it has never been found.

THE HAZEL

The Hazel has always been alleged to have magical properties. The hazel protects against evil spirits as well as being used for water-divining. To stir jam with a twig of hazel stops it from being stolen. In some English areas, hazel nuts were, and still are, carried as good luck charms.

The hazel protects against floods and lightning storms. Some used to believe it had the power of divination, which may partly account for why rods of hazel were used as divining rods as late as the seventeenth century. Even today, the nut is thought of as a fertility symbol. It is also used as a talisman in respect of prosperity.

The nut also features in a few superstitions. In Rome, it was thought of as a sign of peace. When needed, ceasefire negotiators would hold hazel twigs up high as a sign of their good intentions. In parts of Western Europe, hazel twigs became trusted as landmarks to mark property borders. Elsewhere, it was not unknown to throw hazelnuts at a bride and groom to ensure plenty of children.

THE HOLLY

To cut down a whole holly tree will bring bad luck. Hanging it in rooms in the house keeps bad spirits away. Holly used as Christmas decorations in the house should be burned afterwards in the garden for good luck in the coming year. If holly is used to decorate any part the house it must be well balanced, otherwise the wife will be the head of the household all year. If prickly holly is hung, the man of the house will control life. When both kinds are used, it implies a pleasant year for all.

Young unmarried girls should inscribe the initials of their loved ones on a leaf of holly and sleep with it under their pillow; then they might see their future spouse in a dream. Use a borrowed wedding ring on the marriage finger to strengthen the idea.

In some beliefs, holly is considered to be masculine, whereas ivy has a feminine association to it and your selection of either is also said to determine if the household would be male or female dominated. Don't over use holly when decorating, for it may bring bad luck.

THE IVY

For many years the ivy has been recognised as a symbol of fidelity in marriage. It is still used in modern times as a wedding decoration, mostly as a crown or as a wreath. Never use ivy on it is own as a decoration, it must always be used in combination with something else.

Ivy should not be used as fire wood, for that means bad luck to all who live or work in the house. When it grows outside on the building, those inside are free from witchcraft and the evil eye. It is particularly bad luck to give ivy to anyone who is not well, for they will get worse. It is also bad luck for people to grow ivy, for they will always be poor. It must only be used indoors as a part the Christmas decorations.

THE OAK

Peasant families used to tell of family deaths to an oak tree to bring good luck to those who survived.

You may be able to gain money if you plant an acorn during the last quarter of the Moon. Hang an acorn around a child's neck to keep them from danger. A change to the colour of any oak leaf suggests trouble is on the way.

Only cut an oak tree down during an ascending Moon, never do it when is waning. In Western Europe, it is thought that holes in an oak are fairy paths. If you put your hand in the hole, it will be cured from whatever ailment it suffers.

There is a major oak tree that stands in Sherwood Forest and, according to many tales, Robin Hood and his men used to hide in it. Some feel the tree may not be that old but it is still a tourist attraction. In Boscobel, after the 1651 Battle of Worcester, an oak tree hid Charles II from the Roundheads for a while. In 1660, it was recognised as the 'Royal Oak' for its part in hiding him. In some places, even today, people decorate their hats, door knockers and shutters with oak to remember the time.

THE ROWAN

It is thought that to plant a rowan tree near your house will ensure a happy home and help to keep evil spirits away. Where a rowan grows on its own, the nearest home will be blessed with good fortune but for those who cut down a rowan tree, it will bring bad luck.

The rowan, also known as the mountain ash, bears beautiful red berries in the autumn. Red has always been thought to be the best defence against magic or enchantment and this has probably contributed much to its reputation for this tree to have such protective qualities. It is an attractive tree and bears rather delicate looking clusters of berries along with an almost fern-like foliage. Once the berries do arrive, they rarely last long once the birds have tasted their ripeness. A rowan tree is likely to spring up almost anywhere, except that they don't seem to do too well if there is too much chalk in the area.

THE SPINDLE

There are many beliefs just about everywhere that Midsummer's Eve gave people a chance to see into the future. One could wait in a church porch at midnight on Midsummer's Eve and they might see the souls of local folk enter. Those who did not come out would be destined to pass on in the next twelve months.

Should the watcher fall asleep, he or she would also die before the year was up. It is reported that two men who did do this allegedly saw themselves go in but not come out. They are both said to have died later that year.

In some English areas on this day young girls would scribble one letters of the alphabet on small pieces of paper and lay them all face down in a small bowl filled with water. In the morning, any letters that still laid on the surface might spell the name of their future spouse. The light-coloured wood was traditionally used for making spindles, which is probably how it got its name.

THE SYCAMORE

The sycamore, often also called the Great Maple, carries the very popular winged seeds that children like to use in flying competitions. The wood is widely used for making love spoons in Wales. The spoons should only be created from a single piece of wood.

In some Welsh areas there was, and still is, a belief that the sycamore could prevent fairies from invading a home and spoiling dairy products. In several Scottish regions, feudal lairds imposed the sycamore tree, known to them as a 'joug' tree, as the legal gallows. Elsewhere, in some English counties, the sycamore was regarded as unlucky. This was probably because the sycamore fuelled the association with hanging trees elsewhere.

This tree is also called the Martyrs' Tree after the Tolpuddle Martyrs who were alleged to have met to make plans under a sycamore. They were caught and 19 were executed, many others were sentenced to seven years transportation to Australia but were pardoned and returned after two years.

THE WILLOW

The weeping willow tree must be counted in among the most mysterious trees we know. Most of their alleged powers are pure superstition, while others can count on science to back them up, although few know this. Oracles predicted that Alexander the Great would die when they saw a willow brush his crown off as he passed by in a boat.

The weeping willow, such a sad name, usually grows in cemeteries and is said to also possess strong healing powers as well. The bark helps ease colds and chills while some chew twigs to help ease toothache. Scientists in the 1800's became aware of the ingredients that eventually led to the creation of aspirin.

Orpheus carried willow branches whilst in the Underworld and the lyre given to him by Apollo was made of willow. Today, many harps are created from the willow. Scottish folk made cords from the wool of the catkins as a protection against unseen forces and willow has been used elsewhere by making an infusion from the bark to work as a remedy against rheumatism.

THE YEW

In Scotland grows what is thought to be that country's (or even Europe's) oldest tree. Is has been suggested that it could be 2,000–9,000 years old. Pontius Pilate was said to have been born under it or played in it as a young boy. The yew tree is yet another of our native trees. The Druids held it sacred in pre-Christian times, probably because of the tales of its longevity and regeneration.

Some of its branches tend to dip down and can root and form new trunks where they touch the ground. As a result, this may be why death and resurrection in Celtic cultures are associated with it.

The toxicity of the needles may have helped form its connections with death. Shakespeare mentioned it, when he had Macbeth create a poisonous brew of "slips of yew silvered during the Moon's eclipse." The yew provides a tincture made of young shoots to herbalists to treat many different ailments including cystitis, headache and neuralgia. Recently, scientists discovered that the yew also seems to have anti-cancer properties.

FAERY RINGS

While looking at any single tree, several, or visiting a wood or a forest, do remember to look where you are treading at any time. In the late summer to early autumn, fairy rings, usually associated with magic and superstition, can be seen and must be respected as well as feared.

Should you happen to spy one, watch your step and don't break the ring whatever you do. You will be expected to dance in what is left and that could last for days sometimes. Returning back to normal life could kill. Science says that fairy rings, patterns of mushrooms that grow in circular forms, are quite natural. Those who know better, shake their heads in disagreement. I have only ever seen one and that was well hidden in a small local rookery and I stayed well clear until it began to fall apart and die.

It is said that there is a very special faery ring in France that is so large you could build a couple of houses in it, as long as the builders didn't break the ring. Not surprisingly, there are no takers here, for nobody wants to take the risk of breaking the circle.

Practical Uses

THE APPLE

There is a huge variety of apple trees and most of us appreciate that its fruit, the eating apple, is what we often eat as a part of our diet, but apples can also be used as a medicine. They are employed to help control diarrhoea and or constipation. The apple was once used to help ease the passage and soften the collection of gallstones. Apples are also used to help in the prevention of cancer, especially lung cancer. The fruit is also a great help for treating diabetes, dysentery, fever, heart problems and even the humble wart. It is an excellent and well-known aid in curing scurvy and used for cleaning teeth.

There was some early research which suggested that consuming apple pectin for around two months or so might help to clear an excess of mercury build-up from the body. Apples have also been prescribed to help increase weight loss.

The wood of an apple tree can be used to help create small wooden buildings like one- or two-room cabins. In many of the farming areas in the USA, these little affairs are often made for farm workers who may be too far away from home to return at the end of their working day. Here in the UK, some shepherds who spend long periods with their animals use them as well.

THE ASH

During the Middle Ages, the ash tree was so greatly valued that the local lords made sure many were always planted near their castles and fortresses. They were used to create a sufficient supply of javelins and spears. In these more modern times, the wood is employed in the manufacture of billiard cues, certain types of furniture, oars, skis and tennis rackets.

Among other uses, the wood helps to create indoor staircases and wood frames, mouldings for other purposes, treads, tools and/or tool handles. Some other rather useful properties of ash make it very suitable in constructing baseball bats and musical drum shells.

The seeds have been used as part of a pickle in parts of Europe. The young shoots can be added raw to give yet another taste to a salad. The leaves are still used to make tea, while the sap can be tapped to make ash wine. The tree was once used in all sorts of different medicines, partly because it was always thought it had magical and medicinal properties. It was once used by country folk as a remedy for snake bites. It used to help relieve other ills, such as bladder or kidney stone problems, earache, and flatulence, and just about anything else, from leprosy to obesity. Today, the ash is no longer used for such medical ills.

THE BEECH

The beech has been used in many healing rituals since ancient times. Traditionally, the beech was used as a remedy for minor ailments such as boils, piles and other skin complaints. These uses might have been due to the bark's astringent effect. The beech nut was one of the first foods to be used by humans. The nut is edible but should not be eaten in large quantities. The leaf is eaten as yet another salad vegetable. The older tree leaves can be used to make a tea drink. The bark of the tree is slightly bitter and, so far, no-one else seems to have recommended any other nutritional uses.

The tree's nuts used to be fed to pigs back in ancient times. In the Middle Ages, this feeding was institutionalised and feeding pigs on acorns and beech nuts in the autumn was often done in exchange for a fee, usually as an in-kind payment. By feeding this way, the young pigs would be fattened and ready for slaughter in December.

Beech trees have long been used in healing rituals for many centuries. It has been used to treat a wide range of minor ills, such as boils or piles, as well as other skin problems. It is probably the astringency of the bark that has helped with these issues.

The wood has been, and still is, used to help make baskets, bowls, furniture and quite a range of kitchen utensils. Tar from the wood has been, and still is in some areas, used to make creosote. When properly treated, the beech makes an excellent hedge growth that the farmers adore because once it is in place; it stays there – which helps to make it a good marker.

THE BIRCH

There are an extremely wide-ranging number of uses for the wood of this tree, which is also called mahogany birch. The wood may be used to create all manner of boxes, cabinets and many different items of furniture. It is also used for handles, lumber, veneer and as a paper pulp. The twigs are often worked into brooms and brushes and they also help to produce thatching material. Some country folk have even used the wood as hedging material.

Birch leaves, its bark and buds have all been used to make a variety of medicines. It has been employed for bladder weakness, joint pain, kidney stones and urinary tract infections. In these modern times, there is little scientific evidence to support any use. However, it can keep you warm and even help to nourish you. The plant that grows in America, China and Russia is still used in traditional medicines. Birch sap makes a good drink and is used to help make wine. The tree can help to start a fire but pregnant women are advised not to go near it while it is burning. White birch wood bark is often employed to create canoes but this is a domestic skill or practice handed down through the generations.

THE BLACKTHORN

This plant is a tree and a bush and when properly planted out by domestic gardeners or farm workers it goes a long way in helping to create excellent hedging material. Do remember that the plant doesn't grow its little branches to much more than a few centimetres in diameter. However, the wood is quite hard, very tough to use but it does polish up well.

When employing it to create furniture items or making use of it in decorative inlay tasks or marquetry work, the wood is most responsive. More practically, it is quite durable and helps to make the teeth for hay rakes. It has traditionally been used for creating all manner of walking sticks. Curiously, it has also been, and still is, used in the construction of Irish shillelaghs, or cudgels.

As it burns so well, many country folk today still use left-over bits and pieces of blackthorn as firewood. When it is used as hedging material in gardens or on farmland, it does attract quite a wide variety of bird, animal and insect life. In such cases, check the hedgerow regularly for possible damage. Its berries, better known as sloes, are used as food (in preserves, for example) and also in drinks like gin or wine.

THE ELDER

From this magnificent wood we are able to create many small musical instruments. We make, among other things, chanters, pipes and whistles. The soft centres of the branches allow instrument makers to form hollow pipes using the pale and easily-polished wood. It also makes two rather useful small instruments for country folk; the duck-caller and owl-hooter.

This tree has a long history in the use of medicines, from Greek and Roman times, through the older Briton times and on up to the present day. The elder has the most extensive range of practical uses. There is a rich and somewhat mysterious folklore in this respect, for it has many applications, not only in medicines, but also in culinary uses; such as for knife, fork and spoon handles, for example.

We will start here with the cattle drivers, who used an elder switch. Then there were the hearse drivers, who used elder wood for their whip handles. Because the wood is so easy to work with, children's toys like the humble blow pipe, dart gun and spud gun can easily be made from it. For the ladies, it makes beads that can be coloured as they choose and the wood can be made into small needle pots. Elsewhere, the wood is often used in Christmas decorations, pencils and shop window mannequins.

THE ELM

The Romans used elm to make coffins, furniture and water pipes. Elm is a coarse-grained wood, reasonably hard but quite tough and fairly resilient when used properly. It was employed to make chairs where that little extra strength was needed in small sections or very small joints. The ends of boards could be cut easily enough but it was most often used for all manner of furniture because it adds a warm homely touch to a room.

Although hard and tough, the wood from an elm yields and bends well under steam. It holds its form well once shaped, which makes it highly desirable for the supporting parts of all kinds of furniture pieces. The back of a chair, the seat and legs all have to withstand a lot of tension, as do other parts, like the main frame. The wood absorbs all sorts of glue well, holds nails and screws and is easy to sand to a nice finish.

The elm was, and still is, used to make all kinds of baskets, boxes, doors, hockey sticks and window frames. It lends itself to veneer exercises well, can create a good pulp and, of course, it makes nice paper material. It can be quite resistant and withstand strong shocks. This makes it handy for creating many different types of tools.

THE FURZE

These days, many farmers tend to neglect this rather rich source of feed for their cattle, while they wait for the grass to grow. Delays are unhelpful, although they do eventually harvest their hay and silage for the coming winter. Nevertheless, when the grass is thin or scarce, much of the rural country areas is bright with the furze, for it normally flowers early in its usual manner.

For many years, this has been a very helpful source of winter food for cattle, horses and other livestock. However, the tendency has been to not use it, despite it having been one of a wide range of available food sources in the past. In the fifteenth and sixteenth centuries, it had to be registered because it was felt to be so important and so widely used in those days.

Both the bark and the flowers make a lovely yellow dye and in the old days the flowers were also used to help add flavour and colour to whisky. In northern parts of Europe, country folk made beer and tea with it. If you add a small amount of mace and some peppercorns to potted furze, it can help to create white wine vinegar as well as a fine pickle. Furze is also good for starting up fires. Bakers used to (and some still do) swear by it, for many use it to fuel their ovens.

THE HAWTHORN

Common hawthorn has a fine grain and tough timber base and is utilized to make boxes, boat bits and pieces and for other general carpentry matters, such as furniture-making. It is often used to create engravings. Because it is such a hard wood, it can also be used for cabinets, wood turning and various veneers. It's a favourite for making tool handles and it also works well as firewood and in making charcoal, because it burns strongly at high temperatures.

The common hawthorn is still used today as a hedgerow shrub in many English areas. Farmers like it as it protects both humans and livestock because of its twisted and thick thorny branches. One shouldn't eat the haws, the berries, for they can cause mild stomach upsets. They should be avoided by breastfeeding or pregnant women.

THE HAZEL

As well as its gorgeous and deliciously nutritious hazel nuts, the tree is equally well-known for a wide range of practical uses. It is widely utilised for basketry, bean stocks, coppicing, fishing rods, thatching and fencing.

It is also used by many country folk for firewood, poles, tunnel frames and woven fencing. In the countryside, among other things, woodland management involves repeat felling from the same 'stump' (or coppice stool) near the ground level. This permits all the shoots to grow again from that master or main stump.

Hazel provides sustenance through its delicious nuts and utility with its wood for everyday needs. Because of its way of being able to grow back after being cut, it has become a regular part of how the various varieties of wood in this country so readily allow regular basic housing and living materials, not just for the ordinary people but also for organised industry as well. Because it is so easily coppiced, country folk who live and work in the woods have created an industry second to none for both humans and nature. Curiously, not many realise just how much this is the case until, perhaps, they remember that lovely girl's name of Hazel.

THE HOLLY

As one of Britain's most common native trees, holly has been used by furniture makers for centuries. Its dense and finely-textured wood was popular for use in decorative marquetry and inlay work. As the whitest wood, it can also be easily stained. It was used as an inlay in Elizabethan oak furniture and later in the seventeenth century, to form lighter bands of colour on walnut-veneered furniture. During the second half of the eighteenth century, holly appeared more extensively in fashionable neo-classical furniture, either in its natural white form or stained with colours.

As well as its decorative uses, holly will burn hot and long, thus creating a perfectly usable fire fuel on cold, winter nights. The wood also lends itself well to light holders, knives, forks, spoons and wooden cooking tools. Holly, of course, is also another lovely name for a girl.

THE IVY

The ivy, and the way it seems to take so little time to engulf whatever it chooses, like abandoned buildings, walls of all kinds and even other trees, has long made it a natural target for removal. However, in the last ten years or so, studies have shown that opinions are beginning to change.

Several reports have suggested that ivy does not wreak damage as it was first thought to. It is now known that it does not damage where it grows so, with careful attention, any negative problems can be prevented by control when it is properly pruned. In fact, the study demonstrated that ivy has some key benefits to buildings. It helps to reduce high temperatures, and prevent frost damage during the winter time.

Hoverflies are seen to be quite frequent visitors and it even has its own special hoverfly along with the plasterer bee which forage on the flowers as if there were no tomorrow. Once it starts to get dark, night-time moths will come and feed. Caterpillars will gorge on ivy during the day.

Local bird life tends to flock to the ivy in their droves. Blackbird, blackcap, starling and thrush will all be seen during the winter period, and you can also observe scores of redwings as they re-fuel on a winter's day.

THE OAK

The oak is popular with all types of woodworkers because of its strength and aesthetic beauty. For thousands of years it has been used for furniture-making, cabinetry, home decoration and as a structural or architectural joiner.

European oak trees and English oaks tend to reach heights of between 18–30m, depending on their individual growth conditions. Although young oak trees grow fast in height, it takes decades to acquire the body that makes its particular properties attractive for construction purposes. Known to have been used in medicine and ink, the wood also has a special importance for the military and shipbuilding industries. Wars have been fought over oak-rich regions to ensure supplies.

THE ROWAN

Rowan wood was often used for tool handles, spindles and spinning wheels. Druids used the bark and berries to dye the garments worn during some of their lunar ceremonies. The bark was also used in the tanning process, and people used rowan twigs for divining; particularly for metals. Rowan is also known as the quicken-tree, which is a corruption of the 'witchen' tree, as it was planted near homesteads and even in churchyards to protect against witches. Scottish crofters believed that planting a rowan tree nearby would keep evil spirits away. Many can still be seen next to old and abandoned crofts where they still grow today.

The wood is dense and used for carving, turning, tool handles and walking sticks. Rowan fruit is a traditional source of tannins for vegetable dyes. In Finland, it has been a traditional wood of choice for horse sled shafts and rake spikes.

It is traditionally eaten with game, put into jams, other preserves – either on its own or with other fruit. It has also been used as a coffee and is often put into alcoholic beverages. It can flavours liqueurs and cordials and is widely used to help produce country wine. In some rural areas it is often used to add a rather nice taste to ale.

THE SPINDLE

The spindle produces a fine-grained, easily split wood. It is not particularly durable but has been used to make spindles (from where it gets its name), knitting needles, skewers and toothpicks. It is also very good for carving. Spindles are popular garden shrubs, grown for their foliage (the deciduous species often exhibiting very bright red autumn colours) and also for their decorative berries.

Other than being traditionally used for looms, charcoal was made from the young shoots and they were also used in the making of gunpowder. Pegs have also been made from the wood. The fruits (which are poisonous) yield a yellow dye when boiled in water, or green if boiled in alum.

The wood has also been used to make ox-goads and another of its names, prick wood, was derived from its use as a toothpick. It was used by the Dutch and others in northern Europe to make bird cages and pipe-stems.

THE SYCAMORE

Sycamore timber is hard and strong, pale cream in colour and has a fine grain. It is wonderful for carving and is used to make furniture and kitchenware, such as ladles and wooden spoons. This is largely because the wood does not stain the food. The trees are planted in parks and large gardens.

The present uses for American sycamore include interior trim work, straightforward lumber and veneer. Some make panelling, furniture parts, slack cooperage and fuel.

The wood is hard and almost impossible to split, so it has been used for butcher's blocks for many years. From experience, sycamore is often widely used in flooring some residential areas, for it produces rather dramatic looking floors and when used as a colour-contrast border it doubles the effect.

When used for walking sticks, the staffs need a strong hard wood. The strength of the cane would be totally dependent on the strength of the staff. Some of the more favoured walking stick woods for such use are the ash, apple, black cherry, dogwood or the oak. One should avoid maple, poplar, sycamore and the willow.

THE WILLOW

One of the most common and popular uses of willow wood has been in the manufacturing of cricket bats, basketry, craft papers and chairs. It is thought that only the black willow is suitable for lumber. Using the willow for basket-making, the branches are harvested annually when the tree is dormant. This starts in late autumn and continues through until early spring.

Up and until fairly recently, black willow wood was highly valued in the making of artificial limbs because it is a lightweight material that does not splinter. Boxes, doors, cabinets, furniture, turned pieces, polo balls and a whole host of toys are all made from this wood. Curiously, the black willow is also widely used in pulp manufacture.

The willow tree has also had many uses in medicine and pharmacology. Willow bark tea is a traditional tonic for pain. A synthetic version of aspirin was created by Felix Hoffmann. Cherokee Indians were known to have created an infusion from the bark as a treatment for various fevers, dysentery, insomnia, rheumatic pains and sore throat ailments. Early North American pioneers were known to boil the bark to purge various illnesses.

The wood from the willow has been used to create all manner of useful materials for centuries. Its flexible branches allow craftsmen versatility when they use it in weaving or the shaping of a wide variety of items. Many hobbies involve the use of willow wood; mainly because willow grows in abundance almost everywhere.

THE YEW

Probably its proximity to graves led to the yew being associated with the dead. It was believed to protect the soul from evil spirits as they journeyed to the next life. It was also believed to have magical properties, for no would-be magician would have a staff made from yew wood.

Despite this, the tree also had and still has many practical uses. Its wood is strong and flexible and is the best to use to make the legendary type of English longbows, which defeated the French at Agincourt. In fact, it's been used in weaponry for a very long time. The oldest wooden tool so far discovered is a spear made from yew some 380,000 to 400,000 years ago.

The yew can also be a medicine. The berries have long been used as a laxative and diuretic. Quite recently, scientists found that alkaloids taken from the yew have been used to treat cancer. However, do not try eating any part of a yew tree because it is extremely poisonous. Just a few leaves can kill.

Celtic Tree Astrology

Whist researching this work, I was delighted to find all the following information fascinating, because of my usual astrological work. I am a fully qualified professional in Western or solar-based astrology, as well as the lunar-based Oriental or Chinese astrology. This Druidic Celtic astrology, which is lunar-based and, therefore, has thirteen signs, may well attract many readers to these pages.

Celtic tree astrology is based on the ancient ideas of the Celts and how the Druids then created a rather accurate system that has come down through the years relatively unscathed, for the most part, and quite acceptable even today. The spiritually aware Celts and, in particular, the Druids, were expert observers of people in general. As the years progressed, they realised that those born at certain times in the seasons seemed to develop similar qualities. Further, they also noticed patterns formed in the way a person's life progressed. Rightfully, they also observed that the motions of the Moon (their calendar is a lunar year, remember) could quite possibly be linked in some way.

Thus, over a long period of time, the system of Celtic tree astrology developed from out of this connection. Because of the Druid's observation of earth cycles and their own reverence for the sacred knowledge that they believed was held by trees; they have almost always had a very deep understanding of them. They believed that with this, they now had the wisdom for which people searched.

Carrying this concept a step forward, we can associate the likeness and personality of trees to our own human nature. By doing so, we gain a rather inspired insight and clarity into who and what we are.

Birch the Achiever (December 24–January 20)
If you were born under the energy of the birch, you can be highly driven. You have the ability to motivate others, as they become easily caught up with your zeal, drive and ambition. You are always reaching for more, seeking better horizons and obtaining higher aspirations. The Druids attributed this to your time of birth, which is a time of the year shrouded in darkness. Because of this, you are always reaching out to find the light. Birch signs (just like the tree) are tolerant, tough and resilient.

Most of the time, you are level headed and a natural-born leader and ruler. You are able to take command when a situation calls for leadership. When in touch with your softer side, you also bring beauty to an otherwise barren space. You are able to brighten up a room with you guile and can charm the crowds with your quick wit. Celtic tree astrology birch signs are compatible with people from the vine and willow signs.

Rowan the Thinker (January 21–February 17)
If you were born under the rowan sign of energy then you are most likely to be a keen-minded visionary with high ideals. Your thoughts are creative and can be so original that other people misunderstand from where you are coming. This sometimes makes you appear aloof when with them. It is as if you think they wouldn't understand what you are trying to do when you do open up your mind and speak. Nevertheless, although you may seem too cool, calm and collected, you are burning up with your inner senses.

This rather deep passion provides an inner motivation for you as you move through life. You seem to have a natural ability to be creative in all of your thinking. According to the people around you, you seem to make this happen just by being there. Thus, you are quite influential in a quiet way. Others look to you for your unique perspectives. Rowan tree people work well with the those from the ivy and hawthorn signs.

Ash the Enchanter (February 18–March 17)
Those born under the Celtic tree astrology sign of the Ash usually have a natural affinity with the arts. They are free thinkers, imaginative and intuitive. They look at everything in a rather pure sense. Some can appear to be moody or withdrawn but it is probably because their mind and feelings are rarely still. They are in touch with nature almost all of the time and from this they draw much inspiration. People turn to them because of the way they can create an atmosphere for them to associate and use as they see fit.

The arts, poetry, writing, and some scientific and spiritual thinking are areas that intrigue and greatly interest them. For most of the time, they seem to live in a world of design, renewal and much vision. They do not place great value on what others may think of them. Ash tree sign people partner well with willow and reed sign people.

Alder the Trailblazer (March 18–April 14)
Those of you who belong to the alder sign within the Celtic tree astrology system are natural pathfinders. You know how and when to move and how to blaze a trail with all the necessary passion. When you do this, you are able to draw many loyal followers to the cause. You can be quite charming and know how to mingle with a broad mixture

of characters. Alder sign people tend to get along with just about everyone. This is because they appear relaxed and confident.

They have a dislike of waste and are quite focussed. This enables them to see through superficial folk and they don't take too kindly to people who try and fail.

People from the alder sign place a lot of value on their time, which they will not waste for anyone. They prefer to act and get results. Alder sign folk pair well with those from the hawthorn and oak signs.

Willow the Observer (April 15–May 12)
If you are someone from the willow sign then you are ruled by the Moon. Your personality holds hands with many of the mystical aspects of the lunar realm. This means you are highly creative, intuitive (many psychic people are born under this sign) and intelligent. You have a keen understanding of cycles and you are well aware that every situation has a season. This gives you a realistic perspective of most things. It also gives you cause to be more patient than most other tree signs. With your intelligence comes a natural ability to retain knowledge and you can often impress your company with the ability to expound on many subjects from memory.

Willow Celtic tree astrology signs are bursting with potential but have a tendency to hold themselves back for fear of appearing flamboyant or overindulgent. It is their powers of perception that ultimately allow their true nature to shine, and what leads them to success in life. Willow sign people do well with those from the birch and ivy signs.

Hawthorn the Illusionist (May 13–June 9)
Sometimes, people from the hawthorn sign in Celtic tree astrology are not all they may appear to be. On the outside

they seem to be one thing, while on the inside they can be quite different. The expression "never judge a book by its cover" can really be put to the test at these times. These folk seem to live reasonably normal lives on the inside but may display quite fiery and inexhaustible tempers on the outside.

They know how to make themselves at home when dealing with others. Naturally curious with a broad range of interests, they listen well and are sought after by many because of this. In many cases, they seem to have a good sense of humour, along with a clear understanding of life in general. They see the big picture with a strong insight but they don't always give themselves sufficient credit for their abilities. People from the hawthorn sign match well with the ash and rowan signs.

Oak the Stabiliser (June 10–July 7)

Most oak sign people appear confident and have that special gift of inner strength. They superbly champion those who cannot deal their own problems. Oak-born folk are modern crusaders and spokespersons for the underdog. They are helpful, outgoing and nurturing. Some describe them as generous but gentle giants among all the Celtic signs.

They seem to have an easy confidence, as they automatically assume that all will work out well. They love their ancestry and history and many become teachers. They enjoy helping others to learn and like getting their subject knowledge across. These people flourish best in a structured atmosphere, with many going to a lot of trouble to feel in control at all times. People from the oak sign usually live long and happy lives, often within a large family setting. Local politics attract, which may occasionally be taken further. Oak sign folk get on well with the ash and reed subjects.

Holly the Ruler (July 8–August 4)

Holly people are said to be high-minded and quite readily take on positions of leadership and power if or when the time arrives. If you belong to this sign then you accept challenge quite readily with an ability to override most problems with your inborn skill and tact. You don't make many mistakes, which is probably why so many look to you and follow you as their leader. Ambitious and competitive, you may appear high-minded but, in reality, you are just confident in your abilities.

You can be quite affectionate, generous and kind, once you and those you aid get to know each other properly. You tend to skip through most troubles, largely because of the way you think, for you are quite clever. Most things come to you easily but there is a habit of resting on your laurels. If you don't stay active, you can stray into a lazy lifestyle. Holly sign people should look to ash and elder sign folk for a partner.

Hazel the Knower (August 5–September 1)

The hazel sign seems to breed people who are efficient, intelligent and organised. Like holly folk, you are gifted and know how to perform well, especially in the classroom. There is a natural ability to remember many things and you can recall and recite on all manner of subjects that you have memorised. You usually know your facts and are almost always well informed. You might seem like a know-it-all but you are naturally clever and can choose the right course of action because of your abilities.

You have an eye for detail and like things to be 'just so' but there are times this need for control can lead to compulsive behaviour patterns if or when left unchecked. You have a 'thing' for numbers or matters that challenge you. There is a preference for making the rules rather than playing by them. The hawthorn, hazel and rowan sign people make good partners.

Vine the Equaliser (September 2–September 29)

People from the vine sign can seem to have changeable characters and are, at times, somewhat unpredictable, indecisive and a tad contradictory. In fact, this is probably because they can usually see both sides of a situation and empathise with both equally. It is not easy to choose sides because they are normally able to see the good points of both parties. However, there are several areas in their life that they are always confident about. They are attracted to what they call the finer things in life, such as the arts, cuisine, music and wine. They have good taste and refinement, luxury is almost second nature and, under the right conditions, they have that special touch for turning the colourless into beauty. They are charming, elegant and know how to maintain a level that wins esteem from others. When they are in public places, others can admire their classic style and poise. The vine sign blends well with willow and hazel subjects.

Ivy the Survivor (September 30–October 27)

Ivy sign people delight in their ability to survive, often against heavy odds. There is always a perceptive intellect, but there is also compassion and loyalty towards others. Ivy folk are always ready to lend a helping hand, despite their own awkward moments. To others, this can appear to be a tad unfair because people from the ivy sign seem to have troubles coming at them from all angles, often with little or no prompting.

On a few occasions, others seem unable to appreciate how they manage to endure such periods with their perseverance and inner grace. Nevertheless, they probably do so because of their tendency to be rather spiritual, with an ability to hold on to a faith that usually sees them through most adversities. They are soft-spoken and most have a keen wit. Almost always charming and charismatic, they can be most effective on their own in most settings. Ivy sign subjects do well with people from the oak and ash signs.

Reed the Inquisitor (October 28–November 24)
Reed tree people know how to maintain silence at all the right times, which is why they are often called 'secret-keepers'. They know how look for the true meaning and discover the hidden truths, usually beneath many layers of distractions. When the need is there to get to the heart of any matter, rely on the reed sign people to find the core. They all like a good story and are so easily drawn to legend and lore.

These abilities make a clever archaeologist, journalist or researcher. They get on well with most people because they present a wealth of diverse opinions into which they will delve happily. They are adept at coaxing others to talk, even when they have to be rather manipulative. Nevertheless, there is a strong sense of honour involved as well, so any scheming is harmless. People from the reed sign get on very well with those from the ash or oak signs.

Elder the Seeker (November 25–December 23)
Most of the elder sign subjects who belong to the Celtic tree astrology base are inclined to be freedom-loving. Those

from other signs often think these folk seem to be a bit wild. The younger element of the elder sign often prefer to enjoy life in the fast lane and are thought to have something of a 'thrill seeking' streak. When they were born, sunlight was fast fleeting and many appear to behave somewhat similarly at times. Thus, quite a few can often be judged as outsiders because there is a tendency to be withdrawn, despite their rather extrovert personalities.

In truth, they are rather deep, philosophical and thoughtful folk. They are usually very considerate when dealing with other people and will normally make every effort to be seriously helpful at times. This behaviour does not always work, because they may be too direct or honest. Elder Celtic tree astrology sign people work well with alder and holly sign folk.

To be helpful, the New Moon for January 2023 falls on the 21st. For January 2024, it is on the 11th, while in 2025, it occurs on the 29th.

Tree Doctors

Not many people are aware that trees, like people, do fall ill occasionally and need a healer to attend to their needs. A tree doctor, more usually called an arborist or a tree surgeon, is a fully qualified professional practitioner in the cultivation, management and study of individual shrubs, trees, vines, other dendrology and horticulture in general.

An arborist normally focuses on the health and safety of individual plants and trees, as against the management of harvesting woods or forests. An arborist, therefore, is quite different from a forester or a logger.

Once the arborist is qualified to work, he or she then has to learn how to safely work near power cables in order to become certified. They will either become a Qualified Line Clearance Arborist (QLCA) or a Utility Arborist (UA), dependent on the voltage carried by these electric power lines. There are different titles used in other countries for this work. There is a variety of minimum distances that one must keep away from power wires depending on the voltage that they carry. As a rule, but not always, the average general distance for low voltage lines in urban settings is 10 feet or 3 metres.

Not all can or will climb into a tree, but those who do, climb by using a wide range of methods to rise up into a tree. By far and away the best technique is by rope. Generally speaking, there are two systems, the Single Rope System (SRS) or the Moving Rope System (MRS). Should personal safety be threatened in any way, an arborist could use 'spikes', also known as 'gaffs' or 'spurs'. These are attached to their boots with straps to enable them to safely ascend and work. In this way, the spikes would injure the tree by leaving small holes where each step is taken.

An arborist may well be involved in complex or straightforward growths, dependent on the community involved within that landscape area. The tree or trees may need monitoring and treatment to make sure they are healthy and suitable for the property owner or up to the community standard. This work might involve diagnosis, planting, pruning, support, transplanting and treating for parasites or an invasive disease of some kind. Additionally, he or she might have to interrupt grazing or predation, put in protection against lightning or remove excessive vegetation, such as hazardous weeds.

It must be fairly obvious by now that an arborist will be required to consult, write reports and or be asked to give legal testimony in a court of some kind. Much of this original sort of work would have to be coordinated in an office or while out in the woods. Remember, it can only be an arborist who works through the trees after having climbed up in a harness, with ropes or other equipment. However, on really special occasions, it is possible that a crane or a lift might be needed.

As a rule, the work that an arborist is asked to do is not always the same. He or she might just carry out a consultancy while others do all the practical work of climbing, planting and or pruning and so on. Arborists gain qualifications to practice arboriculture in a variety of ways. It stands to reason, therefore, that some will become more qualified than others. Experience of working safely and effectively in and around trees is essential. Arborists tend to specialise in one or more disciplines of arboriculture.

This could involve the diagnosis and treatment of pests, diseases and nutritional deficiencies in trees, climbing, pruning, use of cabling and lightning protection or, perhaps, consultation and report writing. All these disciplines are related and some arborists are very well experienced in all areas of tree work, but not all arborists have the training or experience needed to properly practice every discipline. Additionally, what one may be qualified for in one country might not be the same in others and even then it could vary in content.

The French insist that an arborist has to sit for their Management of Ornamental Trees certification. He or she most also take up a Pruning and Care of Trees certificate, both of which may be obtained from the French Ministry of Agriculture. There are similar requirements in Australia, Canada and the USA. Still more other countries also have their own rules and regulations as well.

There are many different methods for an arborist to wend his or her way around individual trees, in a wood or a forest. They might use a specialised vehicle to get to where they want or they will use one of the many varieties of a small tractor. Walking through a range of trees is one thing but a small vehicle is an ideal choice. It can also carry the extras. This eases the burden somewhat and allows the arborist more freedom to search.

He or she may often have to check out major or minor disturbances – human or natural – both above and below ground. They may be needed to care for damage from a cause they are unable to properly identify until they are close up. Then he or she can provide a solution, such as pruning for health and a better structure or for other reasons. Any or all treatments would depend on the tree and the arborist.

To determine the best course of action would necessitate a full knowledge of the type of tree and its environment. After this work, ordinary people would then be allowed to walk under them again. The technique between the practices of full-time arborists will vary. In some cases, when they first assess any damage they do find to a tree, the chances are that the cause may well be beaver activity.

These creatures are relatively smart and they know how to make a tree drop where they want it to, most of the time. This animal will also chew off branches to build its dams and, while doing so, feed on the inner bark of branches. Whatever they leave behind may be left open and then other animal life can take up where the beaver stopped, or create more problems that an arborist must then put right.

When a beaver causes a tree to fall, it usually does so with a fair amount of reasonable accuracy, from its point of view. What it does not, or cannot do is to make sure that, as the tree falls, branches do not cause any further problems to itself or any of its neighbours. This can create some fairly wide damage that only a trained tree person can heal. It may be a disfiguring affair, a weakening or something that may eventually kill a tree. Those trees that do manage to survive become prone to all manner of diseases, which might result in poor re-growth or susceptibility to a kind of internal decay.

The arborist must now be very careful indeed. Pruning, if needed, should only be done with a specific purpose in mind. Every cut is a wound and every leaf lost is the removal of something needed. Pruning properly now will be quite helpful but must be only what is needed. Any tissue removal must be kept to an absolute minimum because some wound dressings like paint or tar might be unnecessary and actually harm the growth. Some dressings might encourage more decay – causing fungi to invade. However, cutting branches at the right point could limit problems.

Another alternative is to use chemicals. When correctly applied to a diseased branch or an insect illness through the soil it can produce some excellent results. Soil problems are always likely to be improved using a wide range of methods considered to be suitable to the site. One of the most unnoticeable problems involved here can be that of creepy-crawly infestation. When people, especially the young folk, swish through the trees, they may innocently bring up this sort of damage under the leaves as they pass. Adults do not always notice the possibilities here or, if they do, they do not always appreciate any damage because they simply don't recognise it.

At times, there can be often be legal problems regarding the actions of arborists. This may include a boundary, safety problems or the value of an ownership. There are other issues as well, such as the roots crossing neighbourhood boundaries, disease or insect quarantine, along with other disputes. The arborist might be called in to be consulted or to establish what work is involved. What might the value of this or that tree be or who owns this or that, in respect of the potential legal liability? There could be an insurance agent seeking assistance when trying to assess his or her particular problem.

In built-up areas, such as a town or a city, tree preservation orders are often needed before property owners are allowed to work on or remove a tree. As a rule, and in most countries, no one can do anything to any tree without the local council giving written permission to do so. This almost always involves an arborist. A new home owner who has a contract with any similar association may well have to consult with an arborist before he or she is allowed to remove a tree. This is where the views of neighbours would have to be taken into account before planting or pruning growths.

Criminal activity will almost certainly give the need for an arborist to be consulted, in respect of any damage to a tree. They may be brought in when a city or town council or an association wanted fresh plans drawn up.

In the UK, an arborist has a legal responsibility to investigate trees for any resident wildlife. Here in this country, bats of just about all kinds have been given a particular legal protection. Additionally, almost any tree in this country may be covered by a tree preservation order, making it illegal to carry out any work on any growth, no matter what may be needed. Permission has to be obtained from the local ruling council.

Occasionally, problems with some trees are quite minor and only require a small correction to whatever the ill may be. Obviously, others may be in need of some sort of regular work, carried out over a period of time. Both ills are often a tad more serious than most people realise. Either way, these mistakes happen because non-professionals have been allowed to move in to try and correct matters, perhaps to save money. These amateurs who think they know it all have only to make one wrong cut in the wrong place and the tree's condition could get worse. The real problem here is that anyone with a saw can call themselves a professional but only a skilled and well-trained arborist really knows what they are doing.

Quite simply, every wrong cut can be termed as an assault. The tree has been opened up, exposing it to all manner of potential decay, infection and possible pestilence.

When the wrong pruning cuts are made, fungi or other invasions are likely. Also, when the amateur is turned loose, he or she may well use minimal effort to move branches.

This can often result in the branch falling with some of the bark still attached to it, because when a part of a tree falls, it tears away large amounts of the covering. The exposed inner wood now becomes open, thereby leaving it exposed to the elements. One good rainfall plus a few different creepy-crawlies will also attract a wide selection of flying life. These invading creatures can cause all manner of unforeseen troubles as well. Arborists will prevent this by using a special type of cut to stop it from happening.

While we don't suffer too badly in the UK from actual storm damage, a lot of other countries do. This sort of weather can wreak serious problems on the weak points of any tree. Many wounds can occur and while the tree stays relatively safe, following on afterward decay can develop and, eventually the tree will become unsafe. Work of some kind will be needed and the arborist should be called in to investigate. He or she will make their decision after they assess the problems. The most serious of these will probably result in removal but this may require the permission of the local council.

Should there be branches in your garden from a protected tree, you are allowed to clear them away, even if one or two are still actually hanging from a tree. If an entire protected tree has ended up in your garden, you may still clear it away but you should let the council know with a written notice as soon as possible. If a protected tree has been damaged, and safety says it should be felled, then remember you may be asked (told?) by the council to replace it.

Some trees really do sway, which is quite normal, for then they seem to suffer less in bad weather. However, a leaning tree may not be all that good. Although, they do seem to manage well in high winds, and they may even create extra growth to assist in these conditions. Despite all these 'ifs' and 'buts', it is still a wise move to give a tree a 'once over' for your own peace of mind. Do check the soil around the base of any tree because if the roots have had too much pressure applied, they may have broken through the soil cover, and this could now be their 'weakest point', which is where they will require remedial help of some kind.

The Modern Druid

What we know about modern Druidism has come down to us through the years but nowhere does there seem to be any straightforward information anywhere. It is all very 'bitty'. However, despite this, it is possible to blend and merge much of what do have today into a fairly reasonable story.

The modern Druid appears to derive from an ancient Celtic spirituality with an identity all of its own. Most of the practitioners of today strive to be as authentic as they can but there seems be so little to base anything on. Nevertheless, what we have found is that many of the modern practitioners are not interested so much in the sketchy amount of scholastic material – they make do with what feels right.

The Druid of today is a 'seeker' on the modern path and is encouraged to pursue the truth as they find or see it. As a result, it is expected that individual Druids tend to develop their own standards of practice, ethics and beliefs as they move along their chosen paths. These ideals will probably not be shared by all of them but this does appear to be a good place to start if new to the modern path of Druidry. As people progress in their chosen way, it is expected that they should find these basic premises are a viable frame on which to build their own ideas and beliefs, based on where and what they find as they proceed with their studies.

It is interesting and refreshing to note that women have always been treated as equals throughout all of its history, as it has come down to us. Women have almost always played a most important role and have equal standing in Druidry. What few references there are mention Boudicca as one of the leaders of the past. We also look to the ladies who are publicly active today in the community for inspiration. We note Penny Billington, Caitlin Maitland and Emma Restall Orr, along with many others.

We must not forget the female writers either, such as Nimue Brown and Cat Treadwell, to name but a few. These ladies can be found online along with many other women who follow the Druid way on their relevant forums or social network sites. When public meetings are held, the ratio of the ladies to the men is also fairly equal. The majority of female Druids visit several workshops and after many long years where men have had strong leading roles, the ladies seem to have caught up well. There can be no denying that some of these women appear to have overtaken the men.

This is not to say that we should be complacent. There will always be a need for new leaders. In view of so many new female leaders in the general communities, other associations and organisations show that the ladies are ready to take up the baton. When given these roles, women have proved their worth in a very short space of time. It is equally as good to have their voices heard because any negative or passive role is simply not a part of the Druid path or any other for that matter. As more and more women find their voice these days, people are listening and they are being heard and treated equally. It is making a real difference in the world.

Questions and answers have always been part of a time-honoured tradition of passing down knowledge. The modern Druid movement compares reasonably favourably with how they operated in ancient times. It obviously has to differ here and there a fair deal because there seems to be almost no written records to research. What we have to go on today are mostly legends passed down through the ages and what some scholars have learned from various sources. These writings (many of which seem to be quite biased) are of such people as the Celts.

In some areas, the Romans didn't treat the Druids very nicely at all and wrote some appalling remarks concerning human sacrifice. It has never been proved that what they did say was wholly truthful, for they never defined the dead to whom they refer as 'the victims of criminals' or 'legally disposed of criminals.'

The Celts were known to have kept the heads of some their enemies as battle trophies and this remains to be seen as a kind of sacrificial behaviour or, perhaps, their way of creating the spoils of war in such a manner. It most certainly is not permitted in these modern times. Nor is it allowed to possess or play with weapons in public places.

The Druids of those very far off days were very much aware of what was going on around them and rarely let opportunities go by that they could use. They were well connected with the politics and the trends in trade. They were involved in cultural affairs, healing and medicine in general. It is said that it was the Celtic Druids who first led the Romans to the uses of soap. They helped to create new laws, and taught and served as counsellors in many areas.

It stands to reason that the Druids were becoming well-known and respected for being an educated class of people. If one were to draw a comparison with what an ancient Druid practised – what would be required to carry out the same work today? One would need university degrees in education, law, medicine, psychology and religious studies at least. These people would have to have, along with diplomacy, a basic understanding of languages, together with a working knowledge of public relations. It is, therefore, no surprise that it could take up to twenty years or more of training to become a fully-fledged Druid.

Druidry appears to have been a faith that was, and still is, on par with what it is today. In many ways though, it is quite different to those ancient times. It has obviously become important that the Druids stay with the times but without losing touch with past achievements. In our modern world, we have a vastly different culture, needs and skills.

The Earth was not in danger of over-pollution back then, but it is now. While most of us no longer work in the fields, we still don't appreciate the importance of the seasons or the cost of survival when there are no shops for medicine or food. While the Druids may not be advisors to today's political rulers, they are still useful within their community and keep up with promoting peace in the world.

Thus, as they did then, many still serve their local areas through community service. Many have become doctors, engineers, legally involved people, psychologists and teachers. Druidry does not excuse them from living in today's society and it didn't back in the fourth century either. The word 'Druid' seems to have been derived from several sources such as the 'seer', 'sorcerer' and the Greek 'oak-knower'.

Julius Caesar regarded them as some of the most important people in the region, along with the nobles, who were able to organise divination, legal procedures and even sacrifices if or when it became necessary. They were exempt from military service and taxes. They were so highly regarded that they were allowed to intervene between armies in order to stop the fighting. However, when they gave instructions to their own people, it was kept secret, in the caves or forests where many of them elected to dwell.

Wherever possible, Druid lore and instruction was usually passed on orally, very little was ever written down. However, if anything had to be put in writing, the order would probably have used the almost unknown Gaul script, using the Greek or Roman lettering. Starting slowly at first, the Druids began to commit some of their early and in-depth pagan ideologies into the ancient Celtic language.

This might have been one of the reasons that suggested the Druids used Stonehenge for some of their rituals and routines but there is no relationship here. There is no historical proof that this was so. It is just one of those many tales that has just come down through the ages. Wales appears to have been the real origin of the Druid movement, long before written history recorded anything that could be trusted. Druids under instruction were educated through a long system of memorisation. Their law never taught its followers to write down anything at any time.

The Druid movement became so all-powerful that the Romans decided their practices to be illegal. In Roman Britain in AD61, the Romans elected to rid themselves of the Druids at Anglesey, then the centre of Druid culture. While the Romans waited for the tide to go out in the Menai Strait, the Druids held their position. The Romans moved as only they could, crossed the Strait and conquered the island. They then destroyed both the Druids and their sacred groves of trees.

It's all quite different today because quite a few practitioners hold their summer solstice rites at Stonehenge. The Druid movement is alive and flourishing and enjoying a twenty-first century revival with a lot of work put into their efforts. In Wales, the Eisteddfod is still celebrated annually during the first week of August. It must be said that all the modern ceremonies have now moved toward the cultural, rather than the religious type of practice, so that the Eisteddfod remains with its proper Druidic roots.

Just as the sacrificial rituals of the ancient Druids created controversy in ancient times, the modern Druids still find themselves slap bang in the middle of a heated debate.

This controversy comes to a head around the 21st of June each year. This is when modern Druids converge upon what is undoubtedly one of the most visited tourist attractions in England to commemorate the summer solstice.

Neither the English Heritage nor the National Trust who jointly manage the site really welcomes the Druids. The monument, which has been there even long before the original Druids, seems to have garnered a tad more controversy than may have been present at other times.

The Druids have always held the natural world in high esteem above all else. The tree, and in particular, the oak, was top of the list. In some areas, the word 'Druid' is believed to mean "knowledge of the oak" because the Druids considered the oak to be sacred. They held, and still do hold, their meetings in forest groves.

In Europe, many people have held the oak tree in high esteem. To the Celts, Greeks, Romans and many other Teutonic societies, the oak was foremost amongst venerated trees. They felt the tree was sacred to many of the gods of old. For them, each god had dominion over lightning, rain and thunder, so it should come as no surprise that the oak is more open to lightning strikes than any other tree. This is probably due to the tree's high-water content and that they are so often the highest living growth on the local landscape.

The Druids frequently worshipped and practised their rites in oak groves. Mistletoe, probably the Druids' most potent and magical growth, grows on oak trees. Its presence there was believed to have suggested that it was placed there by a lightning strike. Many of the older rulers tried to adopt the guise of a god. They tried to assume the responsibility for battle successes as well as for the fertility of the land. Many adorned their heads with oak leaves woven into their crown to symbolise the god they wanted to represent as a king on the Earth.

Roman commanders were often decorated with crowns of oak leaves when they made their victory parades. If you look carefully, you will notice that even today oak leaves are still in use as a badge of office. Additionally, oak leaves are still thought to be a part of rainfall prediction in much of today's folklore. Indeed, there is a wide range of rhymes concerning the first appearance of tree leaves. For example, perhaps the most well-known, of which this is a variation, is as follows:

"If the oak before the ash, then we'll only have a splash.
If the ash before the oak, then we'll surely have a soak!"

Oak was the more strongly favoured for its durability and strength. It was used in Tudor housing, and artists loved it because of its even-grained beauty when used for carving and other similar activities.

Tanning companies value the bark because it contains a wealth of tannins. One can also create a brown dye with it, while the galls were used to produce a super black dye for making ink. Somewhere along the line, someone also found that a tonic from made from boiling the bark could be used on skin sores caused by the over-use of harnesses.

The Tree-less Culture

Before and after the change of the century there came a whole new wave of commercially based ideas which, at the time, were obviously never properly or thoroughly thought through. If there were any dissensions then they do not seem to have been reported anywhere. Many small and large borough, town and city councils suddenly seem to have decided that it would be a good idea to rake in some extra money by stopping people from parking their vehicles outside their homes. Gallons of yellow paint were obtained and then, all of a sudden, yellow lines began to appear on just about every possible domestic road that local councils had on their books.

In essence, they stopped people from parking either outside their house or home, or at least on the roadway. Not content with this, these same councils also painted single and double lines along the main shopping centres and the high streets that had always been an attraction for people to come and shop. It wasn't just the high street either, especially in London. The capital has always been a wonderfully busy and successful commercial and residential area. While parking controls became more thorough and needed to cope with horrendous amounts of traffic, there came a time when a drastic shortage of parking spaces became obvious.

Of course, London has a transport system second to none, which thrives in many places. To use a car park is preferable to parking on the street because so many roads are reserved for resident permit holders only, whereas car parks allow parking for longer periods. In the early days of parking on the street, car drivers or vehicle owners did not expect to see warning signs re clamping or a removal take place, for there were no legal requirements then. There then came high penalty charges that cost up to £130 with the possibility of a tow-away charge of an extra £200 thrown in. Then the red line system arrived where, generally speaking, one should never park.

Fortunately, this has eased somewhat now and there are a few places where one may stop for a few minutes, although the driver should always be on the look-out for lines, plates or signs to be sure that parking is allowed at that location. One should never expect free parking on Bank Holidays, in the evenings or on Sundays. In some places, parking restrictions may well be present during these times as well. In addition, one should never think that it is safe to park because other people have parked there, or that someone said it would be OK to do so.

On top of all these draconian rules and regulations, one should always make sure that the car is properly and correctly parked, fully within the bay markings. In some cases, the vehicle is obviously parked in the spot but a tyre may be on the yellow line or just over it. Parking meter attendants will not allow that and the owner will be reported. If any badges, permits, pay-and-display tickets, scratch cards or tokens are not properly displayed, an over-zealous attendant will write the owner up for that as well.

One should never stop or leave the vehicle where it might be an obstruction or a danger to pedestrians or other traffic, such as by double parking or pulling up on a corner or on zig-zag markings on the road. Do not stop on any grass verge or pavement unless a sign permits it. People are not allowed to park in bays that are reserved for named users, like local permit holders for example. One must not park in any bay that has been set aside for disabled users, diplomats, doctors, the police, buses or taxis.

During controlled times or if visiting a resident, there are some authorities who will issue a temporary permit or a scratch card that will allow parking in some local bays. No-one is allowed to park in any meter bay that shows an 'OUT OF ORDER' or a 'SUSPENDED' notice. The rules go on and on, with all of them threatening the local or visiting people. The exception would be made to those who offer a temporary parking voucher because of such an eventuality. Thoughtless parking on the highway can cause an obstruction to other road users, including emergency service and refuse vehicles, creating a hazard, causing congestion or an inconvenience. A new Act dating from early 2015 has now eased the huge number of parking contraventions by using CCTV. This can only be used to enforce bus stop and school entrance parking. However, double yellow lines still mean no parking at any time.

Residents were now faced with a problem that was at one and the same time a not unreasonable answer but also a threat to the local wildlife. The vehicle, car or van, would have to be parked on the premises somewhere. By far and away the best choice became the front garden. Nature lovers were appalled, for to pave over the front lawn was not a pleasant alternative choice to have to choose. A few could put their vehicle in their garage or at the side of their house. Removing the tree in the front garden – which was so often a home to the bees, birds, butterflies and other wildlife - became the principal choice for millions

Few people, if any, appreciated what the horrendous real cost was going to be and this did not just mean a monetary matter either, even then. Nevertheless, monetary costs continued to mount up as people re-arranged their properties to cope with this new problem. Around 21 million homes with front gardens were turned into a hard-standing. As a rule, the tree was cut down so more room became available for the car.

The kerb had to be lowered and strengthened and, for many, a white line became a necessity to stop illegal parking across the only vehicular access and exit of the property. Many types of councils charged a small fortune for this. Marked on the road to bring attention to the dropped kerbs, they are only advisory. Enforcement can only be made if the vehicle is obstructing the driveway. Initially, all the homes with front gardens that could be changed were eventually turned into places of hard-standing. For many, the price of this was often the loss of a tree and, on occasions, more than one. Since the beginning of all this, the number of houses with paved-over fronts has virtually doubled.

In a report, one motoring organisation referred to the poor alternative parking provisions by the councils as forcing more people to create a parking space at their home. In addition, even then, they raised concern regarding the inevitability this increased paving activity would have on floodwater run-off. A tree would have helped so much here but without one the then current drainage systems would often overflow. They also pointed out the dangers during these periods of flooding.

Some people who were more than aware of what might happen also raised the issue of not only these dangers but also what sort of climate changes it would create. Global warming and heat waves would occur more in towns and cities. Increased surface water flooding, severe storms and out-of-control fires would exacerbate these dangers that were now appearing to becoming more prevalent.

The loss of all these domestic garden spaces would also present threats to all manner of wildlife. Front gardens are a superbly valuable wildlife resource in any town or city. The losses here would be virtually incalculable. To remove a tree, a hedge or part of a lawn is a terrible loss for the wildlife that depends on it for food and shelter. In just London alone there is a huge range of animals, birds and creepy-crawlies of all shapes, sizes and types.

In addition to these losses, there are also the costs of using the right materials to be considered. When a tree is removed the house foundations might also have to be shored up. Some tree roots really do roam and rummage everywhere in order to properly support their growth. In most cases, quotes are quite high and costs for it all can run well into four-figure sums.

While it may take time to recoup these losses, there will at least be a guaranteed parking place and the property's value will increase if the owner opts to move at some later date. One or two estate agents have suggested that the off-street parking could make or break a sale. A few have implied that in some areas the price may well exceed the initial cost of all the work that had to done.

For nature lovers, to have to pave over the house frontage is not a choice they may want to make. People like this are well aware that they may have had to remove parts that had been home to birds, bees, butterflies and all manner of insects. At the very least, if they are going to go ahead then they will be aware that there are several alternatives they ought to think of creating with environmentally friendly materials. Whatever they elect to use could be quite helpful to their local garden wildlife.

It is also at times like this that people who walk the dog or who go out for their exercise start by walking along a few roads where there are other people and a wealth of all kinds of vehicular traffic constantly on the move.

Depending on how familiar they are with the area, they may seek directions to a local park. Many find that once in amongst the greenery, they begin to feel so much better in themselves. They tend to put these feelings down to the lack of traffic and all that goes with it. It is being within the plant, shrub and tree area that is filling their lungs with proper fresh air that is working this magic.

In reality, this is the power of the overall purer atmosphere that all the trees, bushes and shrubs along with the other wide variety of growths are producing. It is nature fully at work, busily cleaning the area to make everything fit to be in. If you were to gently turn over a few of the fallen leaves, there will be all manner of insect life scuttling hither and thither. Animal life, such as the squirrel, will be bouncing through a few tree branches and the amount of bird life to be seen will really open your eyes if you stand still for long enough. This is what the tree and nature's plant life is all about all the time. They are always there to make life better for all of us because we can't live for long without this generous sharing.

The way all of this extra work has been thrust on to house-holders reminds me very much of the desert climate and the oasis. The location of all oases has always been important for trade and transport in desert areas. Caravans have to travel using oases, so that food and water supplies can be kept safely to replenish depleted stocks. The trees and other plant life provide air where the desert traveller may rest in their shade, well away from the burning sands of the desert.

America once had regions that were important in the hot desert regions. At one time, many places like Las Vegas,

Phoenix, Palm Springs and Tucson which are now thriving modern cities were once small, isolated farming areas where people had little choice but to stop for food and supplies. Today, there are still a few roads that pass through desert areas, such as Route 50 which passes through Nevada and the Mojave Desert and still features a few green areas and small supply towns.

Those who live in an oasis area have to work hard to maintain their land and use water carefully. The fields need regular irrigation to grow plants like apricots, dates, figs and olives. The palm trees provide shade for the smaller trees, such as the peach, which is usually found in the middle area. To grow plants in different layers makes the best use of the soil and water.

Among the many vegetables also grown in these places are cereals like barley, millet and wheat. An oasis in the desert environment may often be closely allied with its continuous passing nomadic travellers, both human and livestock. More importantly, the oasis provides an area where one can rest within the shelter of trees, without which no-one can survive for very long.

Present and Future Life

There have been several serious warnings of late, with respect to the weather conditions we should be ready to expect in the near and distant future. Two of the worst actual weather changes occurred in the 2003 and 2010 heat waves that accounted for nearly 128,000 lives lost in both events. Nearly half of these losses were in Europe in 2003.

All around the world, advisors to the Intergovernmental Panel on Climate Change (IPCC) have informed us that during the past 100 years, the overall air surface air temperature has warmed up by an average of 6° Celsius. Much of this has been due to people burning fossil fuels that release carbon dioxide and other greenhouse gases. This is a rather small amount and may not sound very much until you appreciate that just this increase alone can impact in so many ways.

It is also suggested that during the twenty-first century the average temperature will rise by about 4° C. Were we to now take suitable action to offset this, it is thought the increase will be limited to around just 1° C. What seems to have been missed here is the terrible damage done to the atmosphere, not just to plant life in general or to both wild and domesticated animals, but the huge amount of laying waste to the tree world. If we were to ensure that the present plant, shrub and tree life was properly looked after first, we could then begin to handle the potential global damage predictions with a lot more confidence.

Here in England, we can almost revel in our wonderful countryside, partly because of the rather well-defined pattern of changing seasons and overall weather expectations. However, there is a savage nature which does occasionally strike with little or no warning. Devastating arctic winters, dreadful floods, catastrophic winds, almost unbearable heat waves and severe droughts in England have given us some rather hellish times. Fortunately, they only happen now and then, but when they do – they really do.

Less than 100 years ago, in the winter of 1947, we had a dreadful period of heavy snow that struck without warning. We were still on rations following WWII when huge snow drifts hit, some as high or more than 300cm, with which we could barely cope. Our railways and roads were blocked and our thriving miners couldn't work. In the nation's capital, London, we had barely a week's worth of coal left. In the country areas, the snow was so deep that farmers were unable to feed livestock and many animals died of starvation in frozen fields.

I remember that I was unable to get to school for 4 days because we were so heavily snowed in. Some five years later in 1952, a dreadful mixture of fog and smoke covered many areas in the month of December – it was unlike anything that had been experienced before.

Over 4,000 people died in that week-long stink and non-moving smog. There was almost no wind to help clear the mess and, once it had dispersed and life began to get back to normal, it led to the government to introduce the Clean Air Act in Britain. Then, in 1953 just about the worst storm England had ever experienced on record claimed just over another 300 lives. In those days, there were no severe flood warnings broadcast and all the phone lines were down. The populace was not aware of the dreadful times that were about to hit.

The combination of gale-force winds, low pressure and extremely high tides wreaked havoc to more than 1,000 miles of coastal areas, with well over 30,000 people displaced through flooding. After all this, an official potential danger service began to be broadcast well in advance for the area(s) concerned. The experience also led to better building methods to withstand such dangers.

Perhaps the coldest winter the English people ever endured was in 1963, when the temperature slid down to −21°C and this lasted for three months. During this period, it was so cold that some of the lakes, several rivers and parts of the coastal seas froze. It was recorded that over 200 or so main roads were completely blocked with a further 90,000 or more miles snowbound.

The next really bad weather period was during the summer of 1976, when the unusually long dry spell brought in just about the worst drought England had suffered for over 150 years. Many rivers dried up and huge cracks appeared in the reservoirs where the supply of water almost ran out. Without a doubt, it was England's most rare and dreadful heat wave drought of the twentieth century. Within a couple of days, an MP was appointed to oversee the problem. It then began to rain quite heavily.

There have been a number of other rather serious weather periods in this country but we cannot mention them all. However, in Boscastle in Cornwall, in 2004, a sudden flash flood occurred that shook everyone. The lovely village was totally flooded out. Over 100 people had to be rescued by the emergency services, many from roof tops to where they had climbed to escape the water when the river burst its banks. Nearly 150 cars were swept away and more than 50 properties were either flooded or completely wrecked. How anyone survived still occupies many minds because, somehow, no-one died.

In each of these incidents, no-one seems to have thought, or no-one has appeared to have said anything, about the state of the tree world. It is possible that if they had been properly looked after, the events might not have been as serious as they were. There have been no reports and nothing stated anywhere.

If we look elsewhere in the world, especially by continent, we find we have not been the only ones to have had these sudden dark spells of really bad weather. In Africa, from 1970 through to 2019, there were well over 1,600 recorded disasters that caused the loss of over 73,000 lives, at a cost of more than (USD) $38 billion.

Africa has accounted for around 15% of climate (and water) related disasters along with losses reported all over the globe. Most of the deaths were in Ethiopia during the severe droughts there, in Mozambique during 1981 and the Sudan in 1983.

In Asia there were over 3,459 reported disasters from 1970–2019 with over 975,000 lives lost, at a cost of over (USD) $1 trillion in economic damages. What does get reported in Asia costs around a third of climate (and water) related disasters. Deaths are nearly half while the economy is hit by about one third. The majority of these incidents were related to floods and storms. Storms accounted for 72% of lives lost, while the floods were cause of the greatest economic losses (57%). These days, we don't always hear of problems like this but what has been noted has cost over 680,000 lives and over (USD) $260,000 billion in economic losses.

In South America, the top 10 disasters that were recorded cost some 60% of lives lost, with 38% at a cost of some (USD) $39.2 billion. Floods were the highest and represented just over 90% of the overall events. Floods have been the highest of these disasters (59%), and the greatest loss of life was some 77%. The cost of these incidents has been around 58% for the area over the last 50 year period.

In North and Central America there were over 1979 disasters written up. Nearly 75,000 people died, with an overall estimated cost of (USD) $1.7 trillion. Storms were just over 50% and floods reached over 30%, which were the top causes of the recorded disasters. The storms caused the greatest loss of life, some 70%, while economic loss was over 76%. The USA accounted for about a third of global economic loss created by all the climate, water and weather hazards.

Australia recorded climate, water and weather problems that reached a cost of some (USD) $88 billion in economic losses in the entire south-west Pacific. In Europe, over 1,670 disasters were reported that topped over 159,000 deaths. The estimated costs were put at (USD) $476.5 billion. There were about 38% floods with some 32% storms. In this area, there were some very high temperatures among these figures. It has been estimated that there were well over 148,000 lives lost in these extreme temperatures.

It is worth noting that there was a larger than usual number of break-away ice floes in the Arctic and Antarctic areas. One or two of which were the size of a small country. The warming of the poles has, once again, raised the alarm of overall global warming and what we have to do to offset and ease the problems. While most governments have acknowledged the threat, few seem to either want to or actually do anything concrete. Most say it is never too late but at the rate they are currently moving, one must seriously doubt their commitment.

Scientists from around the world who are on, or advisors to, the Intergovernmental Panel on Climate Change (IPCC) have informed us that during the past 100 years, the world's surface air temperature has increased by an average of 0.6° Celsius.

Much of this has been because of the burning of fossil fuels that release carbon dioxide and other gases into the atmosphere. This may not sound like very much, but even one degree will affect our globe. It has been suggested that the Earth's average global temperature will rise even more, perhaps by as much as 4° C, just in this present twenty-first century. If we permit these gas levels to continue to rise, we will need a pretty speedy course of action to reduce these greenhouse gases to ensure that temperatures only increase by an additional 1° C. The first of our actions should be to ensure that plants, shrubs, trees, woods and forests are being properly looked after and maintained.

Global temperature warming will cause a water cycle 'speed up' because of a higher rate of evaporation. More water vapour in the atmosphere can only lead to more precipitation. We know that the average global precipitation will increase by up to 3% for each degree of warming. This can only result in a future with far more rain and snow, and higher risks of flooding in many areas. Thus, by 2100, precipitation could increase by up to 12%. Alas, these rain falls cannot be evenly distributed for some locations will get more, while others will see less.

Remember, as the climate warms, more snow and ice will melt. When this happens, the glaciers, ice sheets and other ice and snow formations on land may well produce more than the amount of precipitation that is expected to fall. That also means a decrease in the total amount of snow and ice we presently have. Over the past 100 years or so, mountain glaciers in all areas have decreased and so has permafrost in the Arctic. Greenland's ice sheets are melting faster as well. The amount of frozen water floating in the Arctic Ocean and around Antarctica is expected to decrease.

The current summer thickness of sea ice in the Arctic is virtually half of what it was in 1950. The Arctic ice is melting more rapidly than in the Antarctic. Melting ice leads to changes in ocean circulation as well. While there appears to be some uncertainty about how much it will melt, summer in the Arctic Ocean will probably be ice-free by the end of this century. It has been suggested by some sources that our oceans could act as a buffer against some of the expected climate changes by taking up some of the excess heat and carbon dioxide from the atmosphere.

Up to a point, this is good news but there may well be huge problems to face. There is likely to be a much stronger element of carbon dioxide mixed in with the seawater that will create a form of weak carbonic acid. Any higher acid strength in the water will cause more problems for coral reefs and other marine organisms. Looking ahead, it is thought that hurricanes, typhoons or other tropical storms could change as a result of global warming. Warmer surface waters will create the energy to drive away any expected bad weather or could even intensify the situation at times. We are already experiencing increases in the frequency and intensity of this weather and some have brought clouds into their thinking. Warm global temperatures help to cause faster evaporation rates which, in turn, puts more water vapour into the atmosphere, along with even more cloud formations.

Different clouds in one area can cause changeable effects in other parts. While some may offer shade to the Earth by cooling the climate, others might enhance the effect with heat-trapping water vapour and droplets. Scientists, therefore, are of the opinion that we should expect a warmer world to be a cloudier one. However, no one appears certain yet as to how any increased cloudiness will feed back into the climate system. Some scientists are experimenting with models, testing the influence of clouds on the climate system.

Marine life in the oceans will suffer as sea-surface temperatures continue to warm. Fish and many other marine organisms like coral and kelp are not able to move on elsewhere and are at very high risk. We are already aware that warmer waters in some of the shallow areas have contributed to a total loss of around 25% of coral reefs. This is partly the result of being weakened by bleaching, something that occurs as the water warmed up.

On land, these temperature changes and rainfall, along with any seasonal timing, will change many of the geographic ranges of plants and animals. Since most can only survive in a habitat that suits their requirements, many face extinction if their range continues to shrink. Some creature populations like the mosquito for example, that carries a variety of diseases, would probably increase with climate warming. This will affect human health and crop production and cause a possible increase in wildfires.

No matter how severe any storm or other catastrophe may be, much depends on the overall effect it will have on the trees. Provided they are in fairly good condition, they may well meet these problems by offsetting any heavy winds, help with reducing the amount of surface water as best they can and give shelter to the local animal life, especially the more minute creatures like the creepy-crawlies that would be in mortal danger if they were on the ground at the time. Nevertheless, no matter where they are, the trees have to be properly maintained. Without them, human beings can't (won't) survive for very long.

USA National and State Trees

There are now 50 states that make up the United States of America. Alaska and Hawaii became the last two States in 1959. There is a National Tree and each state has adopted a State Tree of its own over the years.

The 50 states that make up the USA are listed here in alphabetical order:

> Alabama, Alaska, Arizona, Arkansas, California, Colorado, Connecticut, Delaware, Florida, Georgia, Hawaii, Idaho, Illinois, Indiana, Iowa, Kansas, Kentucky, Louisiana, Maine, Maryland, Massachusetts, Michigan, Minnesota, Mississippi, Missouri, Montana, Nebraska, Nevada, New Hampshire, New Jersey, New Mexico, New York, North Carolina, North Dakota, Ohio, Oklahoma, Oregon, Pennsylvania, Rhode Island, South Carolina, South Dakota, Tennessee, Texas, Utah, Vermont, Virginia, Washington, West Virginia, Wisconsin and Wyoming.

Following on from a country-wide national vote in 2004, the mighty oak was declared to be the official National Tree of the United States of America. People of all ages and areas chose the oak to be their national symbol throughout the 50 states. As a part of the selection, voters were asked to choose one of 21 'candidate' trees that were based on a broad tree category inclusive of the then State Trees of all of the 50 states and the District of Columbia. Voters were allowed to elect for any other tree if they so wished.

The oak was a strong runner from the start and finished up as the clear winner, with the most points with more than 100,000 votes, compared to just over 80,000 votes for the runner-up, which was the giant redwood. Together with the dogwood, the maple and the pine, these made up the top five. There are more than 60 species of oak to be found in the USA, which makes it just about the most widespread hardwood tree of them all. The oak has an inner beauty, confers a lot of abundant shade and is made of top-quality lumber.

The Alabama State Tree is the longleaf pine, found more to the south of the USA. It can grow to around 35 metres and has a trunk some 0.7 metres wide. It is often claimed to be a cultural symbol of the southern United States, which may account for its present position.

Alaska voted for the Sitka spruce, a large coniferous evergreen tree that can grow to around 100 metres in height. The trunk can measure 5 metres and is nearly as large as the giant sequoia. The name comes from where it most prevalent – in Sitka, in south-east Canada.

The Arizona State Tree, the blue palo verde, is a 12m high small shrub or tree that rarely lives longer than 100 years. It produces yellow pea-like flowers in late spring. They attract bees, beetles and flies as pollinators. Their seeds come in pods that are a food source for rodents and the local birds.

Arkansas settled for the loblolly pine, which is a southern yellow and its timber is widely sought after and commercially important. This tree is found more in the lowlands and swampy areas and, on average, it may grow to around 35m high, with a base of just over 4m. Its needles usually fall after two years unless damaged earlier by weather or insects.

Californians elected the giant sequoia tree, which is also known as the coast redwood by some. It can grow to a height of 80m or more and the widest one (the General Grant) measured 8m plus around the trunk. The coast redwood or the giant sequoia are among the largest trees in the world.

In Colorado, the people opted for the blue spruce, also known as the green, white or Colorado spruce. It has been introduced in many other places and is often planted and grown as an ornamental tree elsewhere. It rarely reaches higher than 23m, and about 5m at its widest. As an evergreen conifer, it is often used as a Christmas tree.

Connecticut chose the quercus alba, also referred to as the white oak, but it is rare to find one with white bark. It is an eminent hardwood of east and central North America. It is a long-lived oak, found in Florida and parts of eastern Texas. Some say that they can grow to be extremely tall and live over 450 years.

Delaware chose the Ilex opaca, a medium broadleaf evergreen that can grow to an average height of 30m and about 50cm in width. The bark is light grey with small lumps and green or brown branches, depending on its age.

The people of Florida voted for the rather hardy cabbage palm, which can reach 20m high in ideal conditions. It is generally salt and drought tolerant and grows near the coast, often in water. It loves long, dry, hot and/or summer weather but has problems with any salty flooding water.

Georgia chose the Southern live oak, the principal name for one of several similar growths in this part of the world. It is a very deep-rooted tree that grows more outward than upward, as a rule. It is mainly a hardwood which is often used by the shipbuilding fraternity.

The Hawaii electorate voted for the candlenut tree which may grow up to 30m and has wide spreading branches. The leaves are light green and can be as a long as 20cm. The fruit is a drupe with one or two lobes, of which each kernel is a source of candlenut oil.

Idaho chose the Western white pine, a large tree that usually grows to no more than 50m tall, sometimes a little more. It belongs to the white pine group and, like the others, its leaves or needles come in little bunches of five. Its seeds are small with one long slender wing.

Illinois selected the white oak, the tallest of which is the mingo, which can grow to 30m or more at times. It is not unusual for white oak trees that grow on high ground to become more shrub-like at times. Some of them have been known to live for 300 years or more.

In Indiana, the people selected the tulip tree, another one of the large native trees of the USA, some of which may grow to 58m with a trunk girth of 1.8m. It prefers deep, moist and rich soil and is known to thrive more in the south of the USA.

The people of Iowa chose the bur oak, a rather large deciduous tree that may grow to over 30m or more and can be as wide as 3m at times. It grows slowly but can live up to 300 years. It is found more in the woods and forests than in the wide-open country. Its bark is mostly grey with vertical ridges.

In Kansas, they chose the Eastern cottonwood, a large tree that might reach up to 60m in height and around 2.8m in width in some areas. A hardwood tree, it usually has a silvery-white bark when mature and produces triangular leaves. It normally grows very fast in its earlier stages.

Kentucky decided on one of the Tulip trees, probably one of the tallest Eastern USA growths which can reach as high as 50m. A fast-growing plant with green or yellow flowers and an orange band that comes alive in April with a lot of nectar, it is valued for its hardwood.

In Louisiana, the winner, the bald cypress, is a large, slow-growing tree that lives a long life. It can reach 40m in some regions and has a diameter of about 1.8m. The bark may be grey or reddish brown and appear stringy. It bears thin needle-like leaves which are dropped each winter to then grow the next lot in the spring.

Maine selected the Eastern white pine, a large soft tree, generally found in the Great Lakes area and often on very high ground. It is known in some places as the Tree of Peace. Here in England, it is more commonly known as the Weymouth pine. It can grow to 50m high with a girth of around 4–5m in some places. It is highly prized and widely used in the lumber yards.

The voters in Maryland chose the white or wye oak as their State Tree. It usually grows to around an impressive 30m, often with a huge well-spread top. At very high altitudes, it may only grow as a series of small shrubs. It can live for 200 to 300 years, with some even older.

In Massachusetts, they selected the American or the white or water elm. It grows well in cold temperatures, sometimes to around 40m or more. Long-lived, it can last for over 150 years or more in places. The alleged 'treaty elm', under which William Penn signed, was said to have had a circumference of over 7m.

The Michigan voters selected the Eastern white pine, which can grow to 55m or more. The overall width can differ according to where they may live. Its wood is often used for timber frames. While not always noted as particularly strong, many were used quite successfully as masts. England imported nearly 5,000 for its shipping businesses.

Minnesota elected for the red pine, an evergreen tree that can grow up to 35m with a 1m trunk. Its crown is like a dome and it has a thick grey-brown bark at its base. The leaves are thin and a dark greenish colour. It dislikes the shade, fares well in windy areas and grows best in drained soil. Its wood is used for timber and paper pulp.

Montana voters opted for the ponderosa pine, which is, on average, some 72m tall and about 8.2m around its circumference. It is often grown specifically as an ornamental in public gardens or parks. The Western pine beetle, along with others, damages the bark through over-eating. Squirrels love the seeds, as do chipmunks, grouse and quail. In some areas, deer will feed on the seedlings.

In Nebraska, they chose the Eastern cottonwood, which grows best in open soil with plenty of sunlight, although it is often found in a natural condition near rivers or mud banks. It grows quite quickly before it is cut down. The wood is soft and ideal for use as plywood or for the inner parts of furniture.

The people of Nevada elected for the bristlecone pine, an ancient medium-sized tree that only grows to about 15m tall, with a diameter of around 3.5m. It has an orangey-yellow scaly type of bark with dark green or blue leaves or needles. It is highly susceptible to fire, and can be damaged by low-intensity heating.

In New Hampshire, they elected to go for the American white birch, also known as the paper birch after its rather thin white bark, which will easily peel away in paper-like layers from its trunk. Moose seem to like it, for many are seen to browse on it. This tree is frequently used for firewood and/or to make machine fuel.

New Jersey went for the Northern red oak, a rather fast-growing deciduous tree that can reach around 28m in height, with a trunk of approximately 1m at its widest. Some can live for 350 years or more in some areas. It is easy to identify because of its bark, which has ridges that look like shiny stripes all the way down its trunk.

New Mexico voted for the pinyon pine. A much smaller growth than all the other State Trees, it is often planted as an ornamental garden tree, rather than anything else. In some areas, it is sometimes used as a Christmas tree. Its seeds are edible and when unshelled they can be safely stored for a long time. For the local people, it is a culturally and economically important plant.

In New York they selected the sugar maple as their State Tree. It can reach as high as 35m, with a typical width of around 5.5m. It loves the cold weather and is greatly prized for its various uses. Maple syrup is one use, while the hardwood can be utilised for many different purposes. Some say it makes a good cough medicine

North Carolina opted for the pine tree, an evergreen coniferous growth that does sometimes reach as high as 80m. It can live for up to 1,000 years in some areas. It almost always has new shoots called 'candles' that the locals test to estimate the fertility of the soil in the area.

In North Dakota they selected the American elm, a deciduous growth of some 30m in height, with a trunk diameter of around 1.2m or more. American elm wood is hard and quite tough and was originally used to make hubs for wagon wheels. With the advent of mechanical sawing, it helped create barrel staves and is also used to make wooden body cars.

The Ohio buckeye is the State Tree of Ohio. Its name is derived from a term of endearment for the pioneers of the old frontier. Buckeye candy is made by dipping a ball of peanut butter fudge in milk chocolate, a treat during Christmas and the college football season. An infusion of its nuts, ground and mixed with sweet oil, is good for earache.

Oklahoma selected the Eastern redbud as the State Tree. It grows to around 9m with a wide spread of some 10m. A short, twisted tree with a dark bark and occasional maroon patches, it has small dark red buds. In the southern areas its small green twigs are used as seasoning for opossum and venison. In the mountain areas, it is may be better known as the spicewood tree.

The people of Oregon voted for the Coast Douglas-fir, the second-tallest tree in the world. It may reach 75m in height and 2m in diameter. A useful timber, it is used in marine decking, railway sleepers, house flooring and furniture. It also a very good Christmas tree during the December celebrations.

Pennsylvania opted for the Eastern hemlock which can reach to about 31m or even more. The trunk diameter may grow to over 1.5m. The wood is soft and coarse and used for general work and making crates and railway sleepers. When it is untreated, it can also be used for making paper.

Rhode Island residents settled for the red maple that grows to around 38m or more and some 45–80cm in width. Apart from helping to make maple syrup, it has been used as a medicine when the bark helped as a wash for eye troubles and as a part remedy. Tea made from the bark was known to have helped with coughs and diarrhoea.

South Carolina voters selected the sabal palm, which can grow up to 65m. It is quite resistant to the cold, drought, floods and the ever-changing coastal conditions. Also known as the cabbage palm, it is one of many species that are found more in the south of the USA and Cuba. The State Flag is often flown at football games, with the tree emblazoned on it

South Dakota selected the Black Hills spruce which is one of many species to be found in North America. Animals like the deer, grouse and rabbits enjoy a steady diet through its foliage, especially during the winter period. The tree is used in paper-making and widely used as a Christmas tree. Japan imports it for 'Go boards'.

Tennessee wanted the tulip tree as its State Tree. It may rise as high as 55m or more and is said to reach its tallest in parts of the USA. A fast-growing hardwood, it is welcomed for its valuable timber. It starts to flower in April and its pale green/yellow flowers yield quite a lot of nectar as the year wears on.

Texas selected the pecan tree, a species of hickory. It is grown mainly for its seed in the south, which produces almost half the world's total. The seed is used in cooking recipes, pecan butter, praline candy and pecan pie. It may also be used for ice-cream flavouring. The wood is used in furniture-making and flooring.

Utah settled for the quaking aspen. It is a white poplar that can grow up to 25m. Beavers, grouse, quail and rabbits enjoy its winter buds. Game animals, goats and sheep browse the foliage. It makes a poor fuel wood but was used in some areas for building log cabins. It is also used to make books and newsprint.

Vermont voted for the sugar maple, one of the flowering plants of the soapberry trees. The wood is used to make bowling alleys and pins, basket-ball court floor courts and baseball bats. The wood is also used to help make musical instruments like guitars, pianos, violins and drum shells.

Virginia voters went for the flowering dogwood, usually found in eastern North America. It is often planted as an ornament in public areas because of its unusual bark structure. A wide variety of birds use it as a welcome food source. Several moth species use it to hatch out their young. Not poisonous to humans, although it does have an unpleasant taste.

Washington voted for the Western hemlock, a large evergreen coniferous tree that can grow to 70m or more, with a trunk of up to 2.7m. It is mostly used as an ornament in private gardens. It needs looking after and adores dry areas and a high level of organic soil or well-rotted wood. It is found all over the world.

West Virginia voted for the sugar maple, which often goes to produce some excellent snooker cues, along with flooring and rifle stocks. It also makes solid and reliable skateboards because of its strength. It is also used to manufacture electric guitar necks because it stands up well to high torsion.

National Trees

The National Trees are listed below, mainly because of their interest – what they are and where they are. At present there are over 190 different countries that make up the world but not all of them have a State or National Tree. Of those that do, there are a few interesting stories behind their selection.

AUSTRALIA

The Australian National Tree, the acacia, grows quite small when compared to one or two other country's choices. As a rule, they reach up to between 3–8m in height, although a few have been reported to have grown as tall as 12m, but they were all in other lands. The bark is brown to grey and either smooth when young or furrowed and rough in the older plant. Branches sometimes appear bare or may have a white bloom on them. As a rule, they grow stronger from late spring until January.

Trees may be harvested to create tannin from about 7–10 years of age. Any commercial use of the timber is somewhat limited by their small size, but they are popular as a fuel. The heavily scented flowers can be used to help make perfumes. Honey is made from them in the warmer areas. If an acacia tree is stressed in any way, it produces a gum, which is often eaten by the natives. Some view this as an alternative to the gum Arabic, as used in the food industry. The Australian National Tree Day is very strongly celebrated each year throughout the country by people of all ages.

BRAZIL

There is quite a fascinating history behind this country's choice. For nearly five centuries, the Brazilians have been exporting lumber in one form or another for many purposes.

The early Portuguese explorers found a tree called 'paubrasilia' on the coast of South America and soon realised it was related to a species of sappanwood that was in regular use in Europe, where it helped to create a red dye. It was these explorers who christened the tree in the way that they did. The name may be broken down as 'pau-brasil' – 'pau' which means wood and 'brasil' which means red. These trees soon dominated trading as a much better source of dye and a very busy trade exercise began with the wood. It started to be called the 'Land of Brazil'. This brief recap of its history shows how the present name for the tree helped to create the use of the present National Tree of Brazil as such.

Among the many different categories of tree exported from Brazil these days, it is a 'red wood' that is used to make cello bows. Another is the 'Brazilwood', which can grow up to some 15m in height. It has a darkish brown bark which when scraped reveals a deep red colour underneath. The bees love its flowers, although people must be very careful, for the branches, flowers and leaves are all protected by very sharp thorns.

The tree is also alleged to have medical uses and helps as an antidiuretic or as an astringent by local dwellers. It has also been tested for its possible use as a treatment for cancer. Over-harvesting created a huge decrease in the export of Brazilwood a couple or so hundred years ago, which led to economic problems. It is now on the endangered species list and is very carefully monitored in respect of any or all of its uses.

The trade of Brazilwood is so restricted in the bow-making industry, which prizes this wood, that the International Pernambuco Conservation Initiative (IPCI), who are bow-makers who rely on the tree for their livelihood, are helping to replant the trees. They also recommend the use of other wood for violin bows to raise money to plant the new seedlings.

CHINA

The Ginkgo is the National Tree of the Republic of China where it is alleged to be a symbol of hope and peace. Chinese monks first introduced the tree to Japan. Then, when a few actually survived the bombing of Hiroshima, they became recognised as a symbol of endurance and vitality. One of these trees was marked with peace prayers on the bark which was noted by the Chinese people.

The leaves can be used to make teas, along with production of medicines and vitamins to help improve the memory. Other quite ancient medical products derive from the seed. For many years, it was used to help ease dizziness, PMS symptoms, macular degeneration and circulation pains in the legs. It is also reported to be of some help with problems brought about by tinnitus.

The Ginkgo, a large tree by most standards, can grow as high as 24m in places. They have a tendency to spread and some can reach up to 12m across. Its bark is of a grey-brown appearance while the stone-cored fruit is yellow-green and rather smelly. However, the core is edible. The tree is popular for its strong root system which is probably why so many are placed in park areas and on garden patios. Its roots plunge quite deep into the earth and stay there. Once planted and allowed to become established, the Gingko needs little or no maintenance or pruning. They just grow and meld into the local area so well.

FINLAND

The silver birch is Finland's National Tree and is frequently found in parks and gardens, where it is usually placed for its attractive appearance with its white bark and graceful drooping shoots. A typical example grows to around 15–25m high with a smallish trunk of about 40cm in diameter. The early bark on both branches and trunk is of a golden-brown shade but later turns white as it grows and develops.

In both Finland and Scandinavia, along with a few other areas of northern Europe, it is used for lumber and various types of pulp as well as for aesthetic purposes and ecosystem services. It is sometimes used as a pioneer tree elsewhere. Silver birch wood is pale in colour with pale brown heartwood and is used to make furniture, some kitchen tools, plywood, parquet blocks, skis and veneers. It makes good firewood, but does burn rather quickly.

Bark slabs make ideal shingles for roofs and when cut into strips is useful to make small boxes, basic shoes and in the tanning industry. The bark also makes a very good waterproof glue and is useful for starting fires. The brushwood often goes to help create jumps for racecourses and/or besom brooms. In the springtime, quantities of sap rise up the trunk and can be tapped. As it contains small amounts of various sugars, it helps to create a rather pleasant drinking syrup.

GERMANY

The oak is the National Tree of Germany. On average, they can grow up to 24m or more and are some reach over 1m in diameter across the trunk. They have a tendency to spread and they mostly all grow very upright. They can live for 500 or 600 years, if not disturbed in any way. The oak tree as the national symbol stands for strength and endurance. The oak is a tree or shrub of the genus Quercus Fagaceae of the beech family and there are over 450 varieties to choose from.

The fruit is called the acorn or oak nut. Each acorn contains only the one seed, which can take 6-18 months to mature. They are covered in an acidic protective liquid, which helps protect from fungus and insects.

The wood has great strength and hardness and resists insect and fungal attack because of a high tannin content. Oak planks were commonly used in Viking longships over 1,000 years ago and were used to produce timber for many years in the interior panelling of prominent buildings such as the Chamber of the English House of Commons.

The German oak is used to make fine furniture and to construct ships, especially the infamous naval 'man-of-war'. It is also used to help create timber-framed buildings, furniture and flooring. The wood is used to make barrels to help age spirits like brandy, sherry, Irish whiskey, Scotch whisky and bourbon. Oak chips may be used in the smoking of various cheeses, fish, meats and other foods.

The bark of the cork oak is used to produce wine corks, while the bark of the white oak is dried and used in medicinal matters. The acorns are used to make flour or can be roasted for acorn coffee.

INDIA

India's National Tree is the banyan. It has several reasons for its pride of place, with one of them being, perhaps, its sheer size. Apart from being considered as immortal, revered and sacred (because of its longevity), the Indian fig tree (another name for the banyan tree) can easily lay claim to being the largest tree in the world.

One of them is said to have spread to just over 19,000 square metres. History books allege one to have actually sheltered over 7,000 men and have over 3,000 trunks. Today, the canopy area is over 17,500 square metres with a perimeter of well over 625m. The largest known example, in terms of overall area, is in Andhra Pradesh. For many years, the tree has held the central point for quite a few cultures and society life in India. Village life and village council meetings take place under its shade.

As it is native to the country, it obviously adds to its privileged status as the national symbol. The tree also possesses medicinal properties. The bark and leaves as well as the sap may all be used, but preferably by those who are trained in its many applications. It has been used medicinally because of its analgesic and anti-inflammatory properties. The bark of the banyan tree is considered useful in dealing with burning sensations, ulcers and painful skin diseases. It can also be used to treat inflammation and toothache.

JAPAN

Japan's National Tree is the sugi, which is mainly found to have been planted around temples or in shrines. It can grow as high as 70m in some areas. It spreads in such a manner that it provides shade for visitors to public gardens. About 400 years ago, an avenue of sugi trees was planted in Japan that still stands today. It is a roadway of some 35km with around some 13,000 trees along its length. A sugi tree often has side trunks, some as broad as 4m in places - probably to provide support because for its branches which spread in a horizontal fashion.

The bark is of a brown shade and tends to peel in such a way that it adds a strong rustic nature to the overall appeal of this tree that grows however it wants to, without rhyme or reason compared to other conventional tree shapes. The wood provides timber for the Japanese and is traded all over the world. It has an unusual scent that resists both insects and weather. The timber is so strong that it is used in pieces of furniture over the world. It can also be found in the construction of bridges large and small, and also ships and tables. The leaves are used to create incense.

NEW ZEALAND

The National Tree of New Zealand is the silver fern. There are many legends, truths and half-truths associated with it. It was first discovered by the indigenous Maori people and, according to their legends, it once lived in the sea. Ancient hunters were said to have used the underside of the leaves to find their way home. They claimed that when they bent them, the fern leaves would catch the moonlight to light their path home.

The silver fern has been the logo used by Air New Zealand. They claim the shape suggests perpetual movement and the folding coil suggests the return to the point of origin. The fern is known to grow to a height of 10m, or slightly more in one or two places. The pale white colour on the underside of the fern helps when creating tracks for night walkers. It prefers to grow in well-drained areas. Once established, it doesn't object to drier conditions or winds and frost.

Some British Army units wear the silver fern as a badge of honour after serving with New Zealand troops. It has also been used as a trademark on some dairy products. The name 'silver fern' is also the name of a class of railcar and its fronds are on flags of New Zealand, despite not being the official symbol.

PORTUGAL

For many years, the cork oak has been considered to be Portugal's National Tree. It is very strongly regulated and protected by extremely strict laws that make it illegal to be cut down in Portugal without special written permission.

This tight control has created many miles of cork forest land with a growth rate in the country of around some 4% per year. Today, it is estimated that there is enough cork in these trees to last for more than 100 years, always assuming consumption remains at the present levels. This is, of course, rather helpful because cork is a useful and friendly material and around half of the world's cork comes from Portugal. The cork oak tree is the only growth that regenerates its bark and must not be confused with the 'cork tree', which also has a corky bark but is not used in cork production.

To manufacture cork, the tree should be around 25 years old. They can live for 200 years or more. In Águas de Moura in Portugal, a cork oak tree there is over 235 years old. So many couples have got married next to it that since 1998 it is now a respected national monument. The Guinness Book of World Records states it as the largest and oldest cork oak tree in the world.

Cork is used as an insulation material, in handbags and wallets and other fashion items. It is also used to make bricks, musical instruments, dartboards and shoes. The Portuguese national postal service created and issued the world's first postage stamp made of cork. Elsewhere, it is found in the centre core of baseballs and cricket balls, in the heat-shields of spacecraft and in wrist-watches and some of their wristbands. This really is one extremely friendly component that seems to have endless uses.

Cork should only be taken from early May to late August, when it can be separated from the tree without creating any lasting damage. The first time a tree is stripped of its bark, the resulting material is rather brittle and is best used as flooring or wall insulation.

RUSSIA

The National Tree of Mother Russia is the Siberian larch. As a rule, it is a fairly tall growth of around some 50m at its highest, with an average trunk width of up to 1m. The crown, which is usually conical in shape, broadens as it ages. The main branches are mostly level but tend to sweep upward in its younger years, becoming broad with age. Because it tends to resist rot, its wood has been, and still is, most useful in many ways. It is especially valued by commercial concerns in open country areas and used in the railway trade for telegraph poles, posts, sleepers and pit props.

It has also been used in many velodromes around the world as the track surface, including Manchester and Moscow. The tree is also cultivated in Canada and the northern areas of the USA. Iceland and Greenland import as much as they can. The resin can be used as a natural chewing gum. Caterpillars and moths love feed on the cone scales.

SWITZERLAND

There is no official National Tree to represent Switzerland, for a number of reasons. The principal explanation usually given is because this is a neutral country. There have been no wars fought here for over 500 years and if ever a country prized its position in the world, then Switzerland and its flag have become the major number one trusted symbol of peace everywhere. Additionally, its flag represents freedom, honour and loyalty for and to the Swiss population, which is made up from four different countries.

The people from these cultures and societies originally brought with them their own national symbols and the now parent country has never sought to change anything. If the Swiss people ever do vote for a national tree, the most popular (but unofficial) choice might well be the Pinus cemba. This is a pine tree found growing high up in the Swiss Alps.

The current Swiss Flag was officially set up nationally in 1848. The primary colours are red and white, and a unique feature is its square shape. It is one of two flags in the world to depict this. The flag contains a white cross in the centre with arms that have equal length but are 1/6th longer than they are broad. Many historians believe that the Swiss flag originated in the fourteenth century, during the Battle of Laupen. The Schwyz districts of the Old Swiss Confederacy used a white cross along their red banner to identify their troops during the war, and that is possibly where the design comes from.

The Four Seasons

WINTER

The countryside always seems so still and quiet in the winter while nature appears to be asleep, but nothing could further from the truth. Mother Nature is very busy where you cannot see or want to venture. It is quite true that winter doesn't have the same apparent hustle and bustle of the spring, summer or autumn. Nevertheless, the plant, shrub and tree worlds are beavering away, preparing for the even busier spring period, when it will all be teeming with life that you will be able to see.

Meanwhile, when you do venture out at milder times or just to get out for some exercise, do not walk on the grass so to speak, but stick to the proper pathways, especially in woodland or forest areas. If you do stray off a path here and there, you could do untold damage. Behind the scenes, in places you cannot see, there may be all manner and sizes of hibernating wildlife. Unnecessarily churning up the soil at the side of a path creates untold damage that can be so easily avoided. Natural water hindrances or breaks by field edges or other off-path areas can become quite hazardous to this mostly sleeping world of plants, shrubs and trees.

If you do go out for any reason, it doesn't hurt to leave bits and pieces of food for the wildlife that are up and about, such as the birds that visit or pass by towards other places. They will certainly appreciate anything that you do put out. It is so important during the winter period, because the usual food sources are very much less available than in the other seasons. Keeping bird feeders full when they need such extras will be greatly received. If you do this, along with providing a good supply of fresh unfrozen water, garden visitors will thank you for it. If you do not have a proper feeder to use, a few unsalted peanuts on an old saucer or plate will be just as equally well received.

Please remember that if you do have access to a pond or pool that has frozen over, do NOT attempt to break the ice, for you could cause untold damage to anything living in the water underneath. An old ball or small log left there can be lifted out easily, thereby enabling life in the water to continue undisturbed while other animals and birds will be equally grateful.

When it's cold outside, you probably put on a hat and gloves to keep warm. Trees can't do this but instead they do have a number of other methods that allow them to survive during the winter. We know that there are two main types of tree, the deciduous and the evergreen. Deciduous trees lose their leaves in the winter but the evergreen (coniferous) trees do not. Their leaves, often called 'needles', stay on the tree all year round. Both types are well kitted out to survive most cold temperatures.

The bark on either type of tree acts as its first line of defence against the weather. The outer layer protects the tree from disease, insects and extreme of temperatures. It is full of air spaces and works like insulation for the tree, not unlike the insulation in the walls of your home.

As a rule, the leaves are where photosynthesis takes place. This is the process that plants use to take the energy from sunlight and combine carbon dioxide and water to form sugars, which they then use for energy. The other process the leaves are used for is known as transpiration. Leaves have small openings controlled by special cells that open and close to enable oxygen and water vapour to leave the tree. As the water leaves, more is pulled up from the roots, one reason why water appears to flow upward in a tree.

In the autumn, all trees begin preparing to sleep and they will then remain so throughout the winter period. During this quiet time, the tree's inner processes slow down. They do not use as much energy and they stop their growing to conserve energy to stay alive during winter. Trees will also begin to change how they deal with water in their tissues. Just under the bark is the system that transports water, sugars and other nutrients around, rather like a plumbing system. There are two kinds of pipelines here: the xylem and the phloem. The xylem moves the food and water up from the roots to the leaves. The phloem carries sugars from the leaves to the rest of the tree's main parts. We call these fluids the 'sap'.

Another way the tree works to prevent ice damage is by trying to ensure how or where ice forms, because it has to form around something. In a plant, a shrub or a tree, ice will form around a kind of molecule called an ice nucleator. In addition, the tree also produces 'antifreeze' proteins and they help to prevent ice crystals from forming in the cold winter weather.

With its water safely dealt with and its leaves taken care of, the tree will settle down for a long nap. As spring arrives and the temperature begins to rise again, the tree will reverse these processes. We see this when the leaves begin to bud and everything starts to grow again.

SPRING

Depending on what you do or who you are, spring will have one of two starting times. For most people it is at the spring equinox, normally on or around March 21, when the sun enters Aries. Weather scientists tend to divide the year into four quarters when they use the annual temperature cycles. By doing this, they suggest that spring begins on or about March 1 and lasts until the end of May.

Neither of these necessarily heralds the feeling of spring. As recently as 2018, all of March was very cold and severely wintry with ice and snow just about everywhere in England, which delayed the start of spring. However, many signs of spring in the natural world do start to show during March, one way or another.

Plants, shrubs and trees begin to grow and flower again in spring because the warmer weather and longer daylight hours helps to make this happen. Some trees will grow their flowers, while others have flowers first, then their new leaves appear. After what seems to have been an eternity – the cold dark winter – signs of fresh new life begin to show. The sights and smells of the new season bring more light and warmth, which encourages leaves, blooms and wildlife to thrive.

Every tree has a flower and while some are clearly visible; others show in ways that are less obvious at first glance. One or two trees have flowers that are green and quite small and appear more or less at the same time as the leaves but, of course, theirs is a different role.

The leaves capture the sunlight, which the tree will use in photosynthesis to make energy. Flowers, on the other hand, help to create a part of the reproduction. Quite a few trees have both male and female flowers. The male flowers create pollen, with the female flowers there to be fertilised. Most folk are not aware of it at the time, but spring is also when seedlings that may have been previously fertilised take root.

Other parts of the tree are hard at work during this period. The roots grow quickly in the early stages of the season, searching for fresh food and water. Branches grow in their effort to receive as much light as they can for their leaves. Water and nutrients are drawn in by the roots and move up the trunk to be carried to parts of the tree called 'laburnum', or 'sapwood'. For the fans of maple syrup, this is the process responsible for it.

Spring feelings affect us all. At last, we can leave home without the warm coat. Once out in the open, the sun's warmth on the skin, the early-morning birdsong, the patches of bluebells and daffodils along with some other early wildlife, all help make the day. Cafes, country places, gardens, parks, shops and other places begin to get busier.

Birdsongs are always a delight to listen to, from dawn till dusk. House martins and song thrushes are especially welcome among all the other noises. Spotting birds flying in and out of a tree will make you stop to observe nature waking up and is always worthwhile. Seeing bees buzzing about is one of the many signs of this new spring being well on its way. Many people keep bees, partly because of their vital role in pollinating flowers, fruit and vegetables.

When there seems to be an increase in the noise, it probably suggests the return of migrating birds. Other animal life will be waking up from hibernation. However, it will be the trees coming out of their winter, with all manner of tiny buds beginning to show, that reminds us that the plant life is not far behind. A tree is always the best place to look to see these early signs of the changing season.

Obviously, there are many differences among tree types. The deciduous trees grow leaves rather than needles and no longer need to make their own energy. The winter dormancy is now over as they slowly wake up.

If you take the time to look, you will notice that the root area darkens somewhat as it absorbs heat from the ever-increasing sunlight, which causes any remaining snow to melt, leaving a ring of exposed ground around it. As the snow is absorbed by the tree's roots, the water moves through the tree to blend with the stored starches and sugars that have been stored there since before the winter.

The evergreens would probably have created their last leaves in the previous summer and they have had to endure autumn and winter. A leaf has been termed as the workhorse of a plant and converts sunlight into food. It therefore follows that it does become quite battered about by the winter elements. The plant will lose the old leaves to grow fresh and more efficient new ones, usually sometime between April and June, depending on the tree and weather. If new leaves are produced too early, they may be damaged if they are hit by any late frost before they have hardened. Should the tree create fresh leaves later than this, the plant will miss out on the improved light levels that help to feed it properly.

Therefore, at this time of year, the evergreen will be at rather a low ebb. It isn't that serious because it is simply the change between the old and the new and is often more noticeable in younger plants than mature ones. The best time to prune evergreens is in the spring. This takes away any hormones from the outermost parts to redistribute them lower down, creating a rather bushy effect. If we leave them alone, they naturally jettison the old leaf system before they start to bud up with new ones again.

However, as there is no point in a tree creating leaves that will be shaded out by others, any pruning allows extra light to get into the canopy and the tree becomes bushier. Sometimes, pruning a tree can seem a tad daunting at first, but it is the right way to treat the tree to give good screening and privacy if it's in your garden and above fence height.

SUMMER

In between June and August (the summer period), some parts of a wood or forest can experience a time of what may seem like wild growth. Some trees may appear to grow as fast as corn, up to some 2cm per day. Their trunks may expand by 3cm in just a couple of weeks. They do appear to be a tad competitive at times, partly because some trees reach for the sky, while others spread out, taking up a lot of room. Of course, as soon as any gap opens up (like after harvesting, for example), or in an area deliberately left fallow, any scattered seeds will try to sprout in an attempt to establish themselves. If one falters or shows any signs of weakness, another one will take its place.

From the tree's point of view, there is no more crucial resource than sunlight. In fact, access to sunlight is often a question of life and death. Each plant tends to develop its own way of capturing its share of the life-giving light. Most trees form their buds during the late summer, around August, as a rule. The plant usually remains dormant during the winter and there is little energy available to grow these rather small but necessary extra growths.

As a rule, buds aren't seen that much during high summer, but they do begin to form in the late summer to early autumn. Trees that create their buds at the end of summer store up reserves to begin the growing process again the following spring.

Generally speaking, most leaves sprout early in the spring and get to work right away. They are like a tree's 'factory' since they capture energy, convert it, and then create with it. They absorb the sunlight, convert it into chemical energy and then make sugar, more or less all summer long. The roots provide the minerals and water required to create the sugar, which is then pushed out through the whole of the entire tree; trunk, roots, branches, and fruit to make more reserves.

This process converts the light's energy into a chemical form. It takes place in the small green grains in the cells of the leaf called chlorophyll. There are so many of these tiny granules that the leaf appears green in colour.

Each leaf also serves as if it were a part of the tree's lungs and 'breathes' the air in through small openings that form underneath them. A tree, whether it be a hardwood or a softwood, usually flower in the spring, but some do so around the midsummer period in July. A lack of rainfall during the summer can cause dreadful forest fires, so people do need to be very careful when out and about in these areas.

Always take rubbish with you and never just throw it on the ground or stomp out cigarette ends. They may not be quite extinguished and still be hot enough to start a small fire that inevitably leads to something far more serious.

Many trees bear a fruit of some kind, if not a seed. There are a number of fruit trees; the apple, lemon, orange or the pear are just a few examples. When planted, the seeds inside the fruit should grow. A plant from which the seeds have been removed will not do so. Thus, the obviously most important part is the seed, for it has all the necessary genetic information needed to grow another generation. Fruit will develop once the flower has been fertilised. Each tree has its own kind of fruit, which may well ripen at different times of the year.

During the summer months, a tree grows both in breadth and height. The branches stretch toward the sky to receive as much light as possible. The trunk and branches will grow to support the increase in weight from the number of new leaves and branches. While a lot of this growth usually happens in the spring, well before summer properly officially arrives, there is usually an abundance of water in the soil.

In the late summer, the tree stops making wood cells and shifts its energy into storing food reserves and creating buds. Early and late wood growth both differ in colour, which allows the annual rings to be more easily counted. Each year, a tree produces one ring; thus the age of a tree can be adjudged by counting the rings.

The tree bark's main purpose is to protect it, rather like human skin. The bark protects the tree against animals, disease, drought, insect pests, fire, and injury.

AUTUMN

Autumn is, perhaps, for many, the best season of the year with its bright colours, along with the retained warmth of summer which allows people to dress as lightly as they wish. There's all manner of accumulating fungi and falling leaves just about everywhere. Plants, shrubs and trees and animal life of all sizes appear in the countryside, woodlands and forest floors to feast on an absolute abundance of berries, nuts and seeds, as life prepares itself for the winter.

With winter not that far away, the temperature will begin to drop as the sun lowers in the sky. The tree's leaves will take as much sunlight as they can absorb. The tree will then allow them to drop when it enters the usual winter dormant period, which is how it will pass the cold season.

This is a wonderful time for the many small leaf creatures and fungi, which flourish best in the autumn. They feed on the leaf litter carpeting the forest floor and, in their own way, help to break down and redistribute nutrients though quite a complex network of underground interconnected threads.

These foodstuffs are then absorbed by the plant, shrub and tree life above the ground. There will still be greenery provided by the evergreen plant life at this time of the year. Evergreens keep their leaves because of their ability to retain water. They help to make the best of the autumn but at a much reduced rate.

The summer weather normally heralds the type of autumn we will experience. Dry summers encourage an early change, as a rule, while a wet summer tends to delay the onset of autumn. However, regardless of this season and when its display begins, one must remember that not all goes according to plan. There will always be something that can spoil or delay the start of the season. Occasionally, it may be the beech tree; or sometimes the oak that tend to hang on to their leaves and misses out the lovely autumnal display.

Holding on to their leaves through the winter occurs as the shrivelled leaves stay on the tree until they are pushed off by new growth in the spring. This usually happens more with the older trees. Despite this little hiccup, the pre-winter display can still be quite a mind-boggling visual feast for most people.

Summertime may be unpredictable, while the winter we know can be so dull, but the autumn period is so often something else. People of all ages still love to hunt and collect conkers (horse chestnuts) for all sorts of reasons. I do it to replace the old ones on my window sills and doorways, which keeps both the outdoor and indoor spiders at bay. I cannot remember ever having seen one spider since I started doing this. An elderly country lady once explained to me that conkers seem to emit a chemical of some kind that spiders prefer to avoid like the plague. I don't mind if a spider or two want to share my home, but this simple exercise really does keep them away.

From around the period of the autumn equinox through to late November or early December, the countryside, woodland and forest areas changes with the colour of the tree leaves. This all takes place out in the open and can be seen everywhere you go. One of the best places is in any of the national parks, where the trees are so beautifully reflected in their waters. Without a doubt, this is the best time of year to observe the beauty of the purely natural landscape.

Harvest time and just after is when many local people gather together to celebrate the late autumn times which are absolutely steeped in so many traditional activities in UK villages, towns and cities with all kinds of various events. The magic of the period is quite catching; pumpkin-growing competitions, enjoying the foods of the season, along with music and celebrations for adults and children alike. Alternatively, this is also the time for a walk through the different landscape areas, woods and forests. Wherever you go, you are superbly assailed from all quarters by the sheer colour of everything. By all means, attend the many fairs but steer clear of rutting stag deer!

Lightning Source UK Ltd.
Milton Keynes UK
UKHW021258040422
401064UK00007B/216

9 781739 973339